# WHEN THE WIND CHANGED

not all soldiers stay in line.

ANNE  JANKO

**WHEN THE WIND CHANGED**
© 2025 Anne Janko
All rights reserved.

No part of this publication may be reproduced, stored in a retrieval system, or transmitted in any form or by any means, electronic, mechanical, photocopying, recording, or otherwise without the prior written permission of the author.

First published in Australia in 2025
by Anne Janko, Rockingham WA

This edition was published via IngramSpark
Print-on-demand distribution

ISBN: 978-0-64-67229-79

Cover design, layout & typesetting: Anne Janko
Printed and bound in Australia via IngramSpark

This is a work of non-fiction based on real experiences. Names and identifying details have been changed where necessary to protect the privacy of those involved.

**For my family**
who let me go with heavy hearts but full trust, and stood by my side no matter how far the road took me.

**For my mum**
from whom I inherited my courage. She taught me how to dream, to feel, to fight, and shaped me into the woman I am today.

**For Nati**
my best friend, who showed me the true meaning of friendship: trust, fearless freedom, laughter from the heart, and a love that stays. Without you, this journey wouldn't just have been different. It could never have become what it was – the most beautiful, intense, and liberating time of our lives.

'We must let go of the life we have planned, so as to accept the one that is waiting for us.'
**—Joseph Campbell**

## About the Author

Anne Janko grew up in Germany and joined the military at 19, in search of safety and stability. But what first felt like the right path soon turned into a gilded cage.

The longing for freedom, and the feeling of truly being alive, eventually led her to break free.

Australia became not only her greatest love, but also her home. Today, she lives with her partner on the west coast, in a house just five minutes from the ocean.
A life that once felt like a distant dream is now her everyday reality.

This book was one of those dreams, too. It took five years, between night shifts sunrises, and honest moments with herself. But here it is: a piece of her heart, a piece of her story.

A quiet reminder that dreams take time, but as long as you follow them, they will eventually find their place in your life.

# Foreword

This book is not a classic travel journal. It is also not a guide in the traditional sense. And yet, perhaps it is exactly that – a small impulse. A quiet wake-up call.
Because I know how easy it is to remain stuck in the hope that everything will somehow sort itself out one day. But change doesn't come by itself. It begins with you.

This book tells my journey. Of a soldier who was trapped in the system, empty on the inside, and who eventually realised that she had to set off on her own. That dreams are not a destination, but a decision. And that freedom begins the moment you take the first step.

It is about setting out. About doubt. About courage. About a backpack full of longing, sand in your shoes and salty hair. About Australia – and what happens when you finally stop functioning and start living.

If you are reading this, thank you. For your curiosity, your openness, your time. Perhaps you will recognise yourself in some of these lines. Perhaps not. Both are perfectly fine.

But I hope you realise this: What you're waiting for might never come – unless you walk towards it.

And sometimes, the wind changes at the very moment you find the courage to let go.

Anne

# **Prologue**

It was one of those evenings that somehow feel meaningful, even if you don't quite realise it in the moment. A mild breeze brushed against our skin, our hair still slightly salty from the sea, and while my friend Laura was in the background trying to curl her hair in the tiny hotel bathroom, Nati and I sat quietly on the terrace, gazing out at the darkening ocean.

No big moment, no dramatic event – just silence, the distant sound of the waves, and this one feeling in my chest that would change everything. We'd been surfing during the day – free, light-hearted, full of energy – and I remember clearly how, in the middle of it, I had this quiet little thought:

*»How amazing would it be to live like this?«*


Every day by the sea, with sun on my skin and salt in my hair, with real laughter and the sense of being exactly where I was meant to be. It was just a fleeting thought, no more than a daydream – but that evening, sitting next to Nati and realising she felt the same way I did, I knew that thought had lived inside me for a long time. It had only grown louder that day.

I remembered myself as a teenager, barely fifteen years old, already dreaming of spending a year in New York – not to leave forever, but simply to get away from everything I knew. I wanted to see the world, hear other languages, lose myself and discover who I really was. Back then, it was just a wish, a longing that may have seemed too big for someone my age, but it was there. And it never truly left me.

Now, years later, sitting on that small terrace with such a clear view of my life, I suddenly knew that I was ready. Ready to change something. Ready to stop just dreaming and finally find the courage to actually do it.

But with that feeling came something else – a quiet trembling in my thoughts. Because realising that I wanted to leave also meant facing the fear of what I might be giving up. I asked myself whether it was truly the right thing to walk away from everything: my job in the German military, my sense of security, the life I had worked so hard to build – a path that many admired. Plenty of people would have given anything for that position, for that stability, for those opportunities.

And me? I was sitting there, wondering whether I should give it all up, just to follow a feeling that could very well be nothing more than an illusion. I was scared of making the wrong move, of choosing a dream that might not even be real – scared I'd regret it, scared of losing something I could never get back. But even bigger than that fear was the thought:

*»What if I don't even try?«*


It was that one moment when I realised I was stuck in a life that no longer felt right.

I was functioning, yes – but I wasn't living. And even though I knew that many people would never understand my decision, I felt it deep down: I had to take this path, no matter how uncertain it was.

I remember how often people told me I wouldn't make it –

not in the military, not through basic training, not in this so-called "tough men's world". And yet, I did. Maybe because of that. Maybe because I never listened to what others thought I was capable of, but always had a sense of what I was capable of when I dared to let it out. I wanted to prove to myself that it's okay to swim against the tide. That it's brave to put yourself first – not selfish. And that the life others imagined for me wasn't the one that would ever fulfill me. I didn't yet know where this path would take me. I only knew that I had to follow it.

And then came Byron Bay. I won't get ahead of myself, but that place changed me. Not because something extraordinary happened there, but because it reminded me of who I truly am when I let go.

If you read this book, you'll understand why I'm not the same person I was back on that terrace. Why Byron Bay wasn't just a place by the sea, but the beginning of everything that followed.

This book is not a guide, and it's not some perfect success story. It's an honest path, full of doubts, small victories, and big dreams. And maybe it can show you that you don't have to understand everything in order to take the first step – sometimes it's enough when your gut tells you:

*»This is your way. Follow it.«*

# CHAPTER ONE
THE DREAM AND THE REALITY

∿

A glance out the window, a quiet thought, a conversation that lingers longer than expected – and suddenly, you feel it: something's missing.

Sometimes all it takes is a small dream. An idea, an impulse, barely tangible, and yet strong enough to turn your whole life upside down. That's exactly what happened to me.

I grew up in a small village in eastern Germany called Burkemnitz, in the region of Saxony-Anhalt. A place in the middle of nowhere, where the streets are quieter, the nights darker, and life ticks along just a little more simply. Everyone knew everyone there, and as a child, the world often seemed no bigger than the fields behind our garden and the little patch of forest on the edge of the village. I went to a normal local school and had a calm but beautiful childhood – full of time outdoors, bike rides, and playing until sunset. My family wasn't exactly traditional, but it worked wonderfully. My parents separated when I was still young, but somehow, we always stuck together as a family. I come from a lively, sometimes slightly chaotic, but incredibly warm-hearted family – a mix of loud laughter, honest opinions, and a whole lot of togetherness. And for that, I'm still grateful today.

But the older I got, the more I felt that it just wasn't enough. Not in a negative sense – I wasn't trying to run away from home. I just wanted to find out what else was out there waiting for me.

In Germany, life often seems mapped out in advance: you're expected to do an apprenticeship, have "something to fall back on", choose a secure career, or go to university. It's this societal path you're meant to follow if you want to "make something of yourself".

Of course I understand that – security matters, and so does stability. But I've always felt there must be more to life. Something that truly fills your heart. Something that makes you feel alive.

At the time, I chose to train as a dental assistant – a job that's absolutely valuable, and an apprenticeship I completed with a lovely team in a small practice. Looking back, it was a genuinely good time. I could have considered myself lucky.

But deep down, I already knew, even after those three years: this isn't it. I need more. Something that challenges me. Something to make life feel a little more exciting. Maybe this longing for "more" had always been inside me. Maybe all these thoughts had planted themselves in my mind over the years like tiny seeds, just waiting to grow – into something bigger, something stronger.

And so, at the age of 19, I decided to join the German military. Discipline, clear structure, a sense of camaraderie , it all seemed like the perfect path at the time. I thought I had found what so many people search for: security, recognition, a plan for the years ahead. In a way, this decision was also shaped by my family – my brother, who's ten years older than me, had already joined the Army and still serves to this day.

He's never been the quiet, grounded type, he is quite the opposite, actually. My brother is completely nuts – in the best, funniest way. Chaotic, loud, wild, but also incredibly strong, brave and mentally tough. That's exactly why he fit in so well there. Of course, he didn't just blindly accept everything – that's never been his style, but he learnt how to bite through it. He held his ground, carved out his path, and grew through the job. It just suited him. Looking back, it was probably exactly the right decision for him. We were all proud when he joined the military, especially at the swearing-in ceremony, when we were allowed to be there.

I was still young, maybe ten or eleven, but I remember standing there and seeing him – in uniform, standing tall, full of pride, and thinking: he's found his path.

The swearing-in ceremony is a special moment – it's when soldiers publicly take their oath, when the seriousness of the path ahead becomes real, and yet something greater begins. For my brother, it was the start of a new life. And for me, perhaps it was the very first spark that lit up deep inside. Somewhere between all of it – between pride, uncertainty, and the idea of starting over, something began to grow in me too. I thought: maybe I belong there as well. Maybe this is exactly the step I need, to become stronger, to change, to eventually... make more of my life. I was determined to follow through, and that's exactly what I did.

∿

Basic training in the military was harder than I could have ever imagined. Physically and mentally, I reached my limits, and often went far beyond them. I had blisters on my feet that felt like they would never heal. I remember one of those endless ten-kilometer marches: 15 to 20 kilos of gear on my back, rifle tight against my chest, helmet, body armed – and no turning back. With every step, the pain burned deeper into my legs, my shoulders felt like they were about to break, and my thoughts were screaming:

*»What am I even doing here? What the hell am I putting myself through?«*

But you keep going. You have to. Giving up isn't an option. No matter how much your body screams or how badly you want to stop – you keep going. You function. I never thought I'd actually go through something like that, and even less that I'd make it through.

When my family came to the swearing-in ceremony after those three months – that was one of those moments you never forget. Everyone stood there, eyes shining, and me, in my uniform, standing tall, focused.

The swearing-in is a very special moment: the solemn oath to the constitution, to your country, to the responsibility you now carry. And even though I didn't fully understand what it all meant back then, I could feel that my family saw me differently in that moment. I wasn't the girl from the village anymore – I was suddenly someone they could be proud of.

But at some point, weeks later, when everyday life in the military slowly settled in, when the uniform no longer felt new and the pride faded into routine, I found myself asking the same questions over and over:

*»Who did I actually do this for? Was I trying to prove something to myself? To my family? To everyone who once doubted me? Was this really my life now? Was I happy?«*

And there it was again – that pull in my chest. Quiet, but constant. Not loud, not dramatic, it was more like a fine crack that slowly spread through everything I had built for myself. I tried to ignore it. But at some point, it became too strong, too present.

∿

I've always loved travelling. New places, foreign languages, sunsets in countries whose names I could barely pronounce – that's what made my heart dance. But in uniform, between rules and orders, that heart grew quieter. I became tougher. From the outside, maybe I looked strong, controlled, disciplined – typically German. But deep down, I was someone who wanted to feel life deeply. Someone who could get lost in a moment. Who dreamed, felt, sensed – and longed for freedom.

Looking back now, my time in the military feels like a life

I lived for someone else.

The days always started early. Far too early. Before the sun had even risen, I stood in line, straight and still, surrounded by cold stares and sharp voices. Everything had its place. Every word, every movement, every mistake was noticed. It was a world where you had to function – and I did.

At first, I was proud. Proud to achieve something not everyone could. I wanted to prove that I was strong, resilient, that I could keep up in an environment where emotions had no place. Maybe I wanted to prove it to myself, that I wasn't just the emotional girl who always dreamed of sitting on a beach, staring up at the sky. I wanted to show that I could be tough too. Disciplined. But the longer I stayed, the more something inside me started to fade. It wasn't dramatic. Just a quiet process, like a flame slowly burning out. I laughed less. I dreamed less. And I found myself asking more and more often:

»*Is this really my life?*«

Sometimes, when I sat in the barracks, between metal beds, lockers, and the constant sound of marching boots – my thoughts would drift off. Quietly, secretly. Like a silent escape inside my mind.

I imagined myself standing by the coast in a van, somewhere far away from all of this. The salty wind messing up my hair, the sun warming my face, and through the open window I could hear the sound of the waves, not the shouting of an instructor. I dreamed of walking barefoot across white sand, a coconut in my hand and the feeling of being free. I pictured myself sitting in a small café in a foreign country, surrounded by people whose language I didn't understand, but whose smiles were enough to make me feel welcome.

I painted the life I wanted to live one day – a life full of colours, sounds, languages, sunsets, ocean breezes and encounters that weren't scheduled in a duty roster. And the more often I pictured these scenes, the more real they became. Almost as if my heart was trying to show me:

*»Look closely. This is what you're searching for.«*

But every time I opened my eyes again, I was back. Back in a system that wasn't made for dreamers. Back in a routine where orders set the direction – not your own gut feeling.

It took a long time until I truly realised what was happening. While they taught us how to shoot, explained how the weapons worked – their mechanics, their functions, how to handle them properly, I often just sat there. Physically present, but mentally somewhere completely different. In the beginning, it all still felt somewhat abstract to me. Like a scene from a movie in which I was just playing a role.

Of course, I knew what weapons were meant for in the military. That was clear to me. But there's a big difference between understanding something in theory and truly realising what it means to hold one, and to use one. That's an entirely different world.

Only over time – with my hand on the trigger, seeing how naturally we learned to aim, to respond, to "eliminate", did I slowly begin to grasp what it all actually meant. That one day, I might really have to use this weapon. And that thought hit me like a cold wave.

*»What if?, What if they sent me abroad one day? What if*

*that's exactly what would be expected of me – in a so-called emergency situation? What if I were suddenly faced with the decision to pull the trigger? To take someone's life?«*

That thought was – and still is, one of the worst I've ever had. Something in me completely resists it. But when you serve in that kind of environment, sooner or later you're confronted with exactly that possibility. You hear stories from fellow soldiers. About missions, situations, decisions – the kind you can't come back from. And they're not stories you forget easily. They're not good stories. They keep you up at night. They crawl into your dreams.

With every day I went through the same drills, I felt more and more: this isn't me. What made it especially hard was one person who should have led, not blocked: my company sergeant major. He was a man who enjoyed authority – perhaps a little too much.

For someone like me – young, ambitious, and female, he wasn't a mentor, but a wall. I felt small around him. Not because I was, but because he did everything in his power to make me feel that way. Mistakes were hunted down. Respect was absent. It felt as if he took every opportunity to put obstacles in my way.

And yet – as strange as it sounds, he brought me closer to my real goal. Not because he meant to, but precisely because he showed me, day after day, how wrong I was here. His behaviour left a deep mark, not as weakness in me, but as a clear reflection of what I no longer wanted. He wasn't a roadblock. He was a signpost. Pointing me in a different direction.

At some point, the scheduled course came up – a shooting exercise I was required to repeat. And of all people, it was with him. A whole week. I knew: I couldn't do it. I didn't want to, and simply couldn't, spend that time with someone who systematically made me feel small. So I did everything I could to avoid it – and it worked.

Back then, I only felt relief. But what I didn't know: skipping that course would change my life.

The letter said my contract would be reviewed. Because I hadn't taken part in the training, my military commitment had to be reassessed. I was given two options: either retake the course at a later date, or agree to a shortened period of service. I sat there for a long time, with the letter in my hand. I read those lines over and over, as if I had to make sure I was reading them correctly.

Could this really be happening? After all those months of feeling trapped, something that had seemed set in stone suddenly began to shift. All of a sudden, there it was – a door. Not wide open, but slightly ajar. And I could see through it. To what I had dreamed of for so long.

Freedom. Air. Uncertainty – but also possibility. This was my chance. And still, it wasn't easy.

I thought about all the time I had already invested. The effort, the pride of my family, everything I had built, step by step, with aching feet, sleepless nights, and clenched teeth.

Was it right to just leave all of that behind? I don't know how long it really took me to decide. But at some point, it became so clear inside me that I couldn't question it anymore.

*I signed. Shaking, but certain.*

I had agreed to end my service. And with each day that passed, it became clearer: this was really happening.

The uniform, the structure, the familiar – I was going to leave it behind. Not out of weakness. But because I was finally ready to follow what, for the first time in a long while, truly felt right again: my heart.

## CHAPTER TWO
MAYBE IT'S TIME

That same evening, after I had actually signed the request to shorten my service during the day at work, I picked up the phone and called Nati. My heart was beating faster than usual as I waited for her to answer – and the moment I heard her voice, tears welled up in my eyes. Not from sadness, but from pure, overwhelming relief.

» *I did it,*« I said quietly, my voice trembling slightly.
»*I really signed it.*«

There was a moment of silence on the other end, but it wasn't an uncomfortable silence. It was one of those rare, meaningful pauses where no words are needed, because you understand each other completely without speaking. Then I heard her smile. I could hear it even before she said a word You could feel the excitement in her voice, and both of us knew exactly what this meant. This was the first real step. No longer just an idea, a thought, a plan – but the true beginning of our dream.

We were excited, full of anticipation, full of energy, and at the same time speechless that this dream was suddenly within reach. We chatted for hours that evening. About Australia, about everything that lay ahead. About the next steps, what Nati still had to sort out at work, how we wanted to approach it all, and who we should tell first.

The next day, one thing was clear for both of us: we wanted to share the news with someone very special – my mum.

The moment we stood at her front door felt just as exciting as it did slightly mad. When she opened the door and saw us, we both said in unison:

*»We have something to tell you.«*

But before we could even get a word out, she replied – in that typical, dry manner I love so much:

*»You're going abroad for a year!«*

For a second we were speechless, and then we all burst out laughing. Of course, she had a million questions.

*»What exactly are you planning? What kind of work will you do? Will you buy a car? Where will you live?«*

And the more she asked, the more I realised: I didn't want to plan everything. For the first time in my life, the unknown didn't feel threatening – it felt like freedom.

But not everyone was as convinced as we were. My grandparents, for example, they stood there as if I'd just announced I was moving to Mars. And then there was me, their granddaughter, standing there with glowing eyes, saying:

*»I don't have a solid plan yet. I'm just going.«*

As much as everyone worried – my family wouldn't be my family if they weren't at least a little bit crazy themselves.

Telling them about our plan made me realise, perhaps for the first time, what this step truly meant. It wasn't just a change of scenery. It wasn't a holiday for a few weeks. It was a radical new beginning. A clean cut.

I sat there, full of excitement, but with a lump in my throat. Because to start a new chapter in Australia, I first had to close the old one.

There was my car – a brand-new one I absolutely loved. My little piece of freedom. There were my furniture – carefully chosen, piece by piece. And there was my flat – not just any flat, but my first real dream apartment. A place that, for the first time, had felt like home. A sanctuary I had furnished with love and filled with memories. But now, everything had to go.

I also knew I had to find a new tenant as soon as possible. I didn't want to just leave it up to my landlord – who knew how long he'd take to find someone willing to take over everything? So I decided to take matters into my own hands. As it turned out, I was incredibly lucky: a colleague of mine mentioned that a friend of hers was urgently looking for a flat.

We arranged to meet, I showed him my little place, and he immediately fell in love with it. He wanted everything – the entire setup, from the sofa to the lamp. It felt as if the universe understood that I was ready to let go. As if this exact moment had been meant for me.

I still remember the day I packed my moving boxes. I brought them to my mum's place – they'd be waiting for me there. Safely stored. Maybe just for a few months. Maybe for years. Or maybe even forever.

A few weeks later came the handover. I walked through each room one last time, took a deep breath, let my eyes wander. I thought I would cry. But strangely, there was only calm. A quiet farewell. And instead of tears, there was this soft, grateful feeling. Not because it was easy, but because I knew I was letting go to begin something new. Something I had wished for, for so long.

After handing over the keys, it was clear: there was no turning back. So I had to think of everything. I cancelled every remaining contract, changed my address, and sorted out everything still left to do. I officially registered my mum's address as my new place of residence – because I wasn't leaving Germany forever. Not yet, at least.

It wasn't a permanent move, because I was going to Australia on a Work & Holiday visa.

Still, my whole life was now shifting somewhere else. I cancelled my phone contract, paused insurance policies, and ended memberships I wouldn't need anymore.

Everything that had quietly accumulated over the years – all those small subscriptions and automatic deductions, now stepped into the spotlight and needed attention. I combed through my bank statements to make sure I wouldn't miss any payments. I thought about what would happen with my mail, set up mail forwarding, informed banks, health insurance, government offices. I had to find out what I could cancel, and what I had to keep to avoid problems later on.

One of the biggest items on my list, however, was my car. My little new car, my loyal companion, my personal slice of freedom. Selling it honestly wasn't easy for me. But I knew it had to be done. Luckily, I quickly found someone I trusted – an acquaintance I had known for a long time. I knew she'd take good care of it, and that made it easier to let go.

It was a strange mix of letting go and running a full-on bureaucracy marathon. Every single day brought something new: a form to fill in, a deadline to meet, a phone number that led to endless hold music. And of course, there was the big question on my mind:

*»What can I take to Australia – and what not?«*

I started writing lists. Ticking things off. Sometimes it felt like I was spending more time dismantling my life in Germany than looking forward to what was ahead. But that was exactly what had to be done. Before you can truly let go, you have to say a proper goodbye, even to the small, invisible things. Only once everything is taken care of can you fully focus your energy on the next big steps – the flight, the planning, the visa, the dream.

And then it came – that one, very special day.

I drove through the barracks gate one last time – a place that had been part of my everyday life for years.

As I sat in the car and glanced into the rear-view mirror, the song "Maybe it's time to let the old ways die" by Bradley Cooper started playing on the radio. In that moment, I couldn't hold it in anymore. Tears welled up in my eyes. It was all too much. The thought that I was really, finally closing this chapter hit me straight in the heart. It felt as though a massive weight had been lifted from me – not just symbolically, but physically. Everything I had carried for so long – expectations, pressure, a life that didn't fit me, started to fall away, piece by piece.

That very evening, I booked the flights. The decision had been made – and shortly afterwards, the message arrived: our visa had been approved.

Nati and I could hardly believe it. We jumped around, laughed, screamed with joy. It was official!

A few days later, my farewell party took place – organised by my mum. The garden was decorated with Australia signs, kangaroo balloons, and little nods to what lay ahead.

The most emotional moment? Without question: the letters from my parents. Both of them had written to me – pages and pages, handwritten, filled with words that hit me straight in the heart. Especially my mum's letter, was so full of warmth, closeness, and those gentle, honest thoughts only a mother can put into words. Every line felt like a loving hug from afar, like a quiet

*»I'm with you.«*

Even though the farewell was approaching, her words felt close. She wrote about her worries, her pride, everything she wanted to send me off with – and as I read, the tears quietly rolled down my cheeks.

Then came the letter from my dad. He had sat down too, filling page after page, with thoughts, memories, and wishes for my journey. It was honest, deep, and full of love, and I could barely read a paragraph without needing to pause. That was the moment I truly realised what I was leaving behind. One part of his letter has stayed with me more than anything else:

*»Little girl, my little girl.*
*Take care, little Anne. I will miss you deeply, and not just me. We will all miss you.*
*I wish you all the very best once again. Make the most of it, always take care of yourself, stay healthy… and dance with the sharks.*

*With love, your dad.«*

Those words burned themselves into my heart. I carried them with me – not just in my suitcase, but deep within. Every time I felt lost or homesick, I would bring them back to mind. Because that's exactly what it was: love, courage, and a gentle push into the unknown. And even though it hurt, I knew this was the right decision.

But before things got truly serious, we organised one more small farewell gathering with friends – no big fuss, but full of heart. Everyone was genuinely happy for us. You could feel the excitement, the anticipation – not just in us, but in all the people who had been part of our lives in recent years.

That evening, we sat around the campfire for hours. It was one of those nights where the conversations just wouldn't end, where the fire crackled and everyone wanted to share something close to their heart. Our friends asked us countless questions, and some of them we couldn't even answer ourselves.

*»What will you do over there? How long are you staying? Where will you sleep? How does it feel? Aren't you*

*nervous?«*

Many of them couldn't imagine doing something like this themselves, and that made it even more special for us. Because even though not everyone would have chosen this path, they all stood behind us. You could feel that they were proud. And that kind of support, that warm sense of encouragement, gave us even more confidence in what lay ahead.

The final days were approaching. Slowly, I started packing. No suitcase. No elegant little bag with wheels that you could roll effortlessly behind you. No, it had to be a backpack. But not just any backpack. It was one that felt bigger than me, bulky, heavy, awkward, and just looking at it felt like a small life challenge. The weight on my back was all too familiar. Thanks to all the marches during my time in the military, I knew exactly what to expect. Back then, it was 15 kilos on my shoulders, a rifle in front – and off we went, hour after hour. I had hated it.

I still remember the burning in my shoulders, the blisters on my feet, the feeling of suffocating under the helmet.

And now? Now I was standing there with a different backpack but the same weight, and I couldn't help but grin. How funny is that? I'm leaving the military because I wanted to get away from exactly these things, and here I am, choosing a lifestyle where I'm once again strapping a giant pack to my back. Only this time, I'm doing it willingly. Not because I have to, but because I want to.

The first time I tried to lift it, I had to brace myself just to get it off the ground. And once it was on my back, there was barely any of me left to see – just one huge, overstuffed backpack on two legs. My head barely stuck out above it. Anyone who saw me like that had to laugh, including me. I tried to cram in everything I thought I might need for the journey ahead. Clothes, a few keepsakes, practical things. Things I believed would give me a sense of stability in a world I didn't even know yet.

The days passed faster than I could grasp, and suddenly it was here – that day, that moment where excitement and the pain of goodbye go hand in hand.

Together with my loved ones, I made my way to the airport in Berlin. My heart was racing. The goodbye was getting closer. Only: Nati wasn't there yet. She was on her way with our friend Lena who – being Lena – stopped for a cigarette on the way. Then came traffic, then a missed exit. I waited anxiously inside the airport, checking the time again and again. But then – finally, they showed up. Out of breath, but just in time.

For Nati, saying goodbye was especially hard. She had to part from Eric, her partner, her anchor, her calm in the storm. The two of them had one of those rare relationships – not loud, but deep. Built on trust, respect, and honest connection. I had always admired their love.

He didn't try to hold her back, made no demands, caused no drama. He let her go, with nothing but love in her bag. And to me, that was true strength.

As we all hugged, through tears, airport noise, muddled announcements and those last shared glances – it hit me with full force: this is really happening. From now on, everything will be different. A new chapter. A real new beginning.

I hugged my mum one last time – tight, as if we could freeze the moment, hold back time for just a little longer before everything started. I could feel her holding me as if she wanted to pass on all her strength and protection, for this big step that she supported with tears in her eyes, but with nothing but love in her heart.

My best friends were there too, my family, people who had carried me through years of life. We already had headaches from crying so much, red eyes, and sore voices from all the farewells. But still, everyone stood there, smiling as best they could. One last group photo was taken. All together. A chaotic shot where nearly everyone looked puffy-eyed or tear-stained, but that's what made it so beautiful. A real picture. One that wasn't posed but truly captured what we were all feeling.

I promised my mum I'd come home safe and happy. And I meant it. Even if she knew I wasn't always the most sensible one… and neither was Nati. We were always up to something. She knew that better than anyone. But maybe that's exactly why she couldn't help but smile, even with glassy eyes and a lump in her throat.

And then the time had come. We stepped up to the check-in counter. Our passports shook slightly in our hands, the visas were checked, and the boarding passes printed. A soft beep, a confirming nod,  and there it was: the gate to everything we had dreamed about for so long.

We handed over our enormous backpacks. They were far too heavy, far too bulky, and yet they contained everything we would need from that moment on. As they were placed onto the baggage belt, I found myself watching them with a hint of nostalgia. Somehow, this was the moment when there was truly no turning back. We turned around one last time and looked at the sad, but loving faces that were saying goodbye.

And right then, Nati and I burst into tears – not out of fear, but from being completely overwhelmed. It was that enormous, hard-to-grasp feeling when farewell, departure, letting go and excitement all come together in one single moment. Our hearts were pounding loudly, as if they somehow knew that something fundamental was about to change. We had no idea what lay ahead, and that's exactly what made it feel so intense. It was bittersweet, like a chapter that was closing while the next one already lay open in front of us.

Now it was time for Australia, and for a 25-hour flight. With racing hearts, tear-streaked cheeks, and the quiet knowledge:

*we were doing the bravest thing we had ever done.*

# CHAPTER THREE
## LANDING IN FREEDOM

It took 25 hours until we finally arrived in tropical northern Australia – in Cairns. Twenty-five hours in which the world beneath us blurred and our old life slowly faded away.

I love flying. Not the hours of sitting, I hate that with a passion. My legs ached, my neck was stiff, and at least every three hours I wondered if it would ever end. But even with all of that, I still love it. I love that feeling when the wheels lift off the ground, when you leave everything familiar behind and suddenly float above the clouds – weightless, free.

If you've never seen a sunrise from 10,000 metres above, watched the light and shadows dance in soft pastels while entire continents sleep below you – then you've truly missed something. Maybe even those who are terrified of flying would change their minds if they experienced just that one moment. It's as if you're seeing the world with new eyes. As if you suddenly realise how vast it really is, and how small we are in comparison, with all our fears, doubts and dreams.

The last two hours of the flight were the most exciting. As we slowly drifted over northern Australia, I was glued to the window. Below us stretched a lush green bush landscape that seemed to go on forever. Then suddenly – the sea. Turquoise, wild, breathtaking. Palm trees, mangroves, and winding coastlines, like someone had painted a masterpiece just for us. I could feel my heart racing, my hands turning clammy. It was really happening. This wasn't a dream anymore – we were actually landing on another continent. On an island halfway across the world from everything we knew.

When we finally landed and the aircraft doors opened, we were hit by hot, heavy air –humid and tropical, unlike anything we'd ever known. We were completely exhausted, our eyes burning, our heads foggy. In that moment, someone could've dropped us into any random country and we probably would've believed it. But then we heard the first voices around us. And there it was – the famous Aussie accent.

Before the trip, I had bravely studied vocabulary with a language app, listened to sample conversations, even tried to memorise a few useful phrases. But nothing had prepared me for this.

Australians don't speak English. At least not the kind you learn at school. They speak fast, swallow half the words, and stick "ie" or "o" onto everything like it's completely normal. A few examples?

"Afternoon" becomes "arvo", "breakfast" turns into "brekkie", "McDonald's" becomes "Maccas", and "sunglasses"? Of course – "sunnies".

Nati and I looked at each other, two completely overwhelmed backpackers on their first day at school in a foreign world. We stood in the airport, no idea how to get to our hostel, our bodies in full jetlag mode, our backpacks heavy on our shoulders.

At the information desk, we tried with our broken English. Just to be safe, we pulled out Google Translate, and still only understood half of what was said. But the woman at the desk was incredibly kind. She spoke slowly, smiled the entire time as if she could sense how overwhelmed we were, and patiently explained how to find the right shuttle bus.

So our very first impression was already overwhelming – not just because of the landscape, but because of the people. So many Aussies radiated a warmth I had rarely experienced anywhere else. Their relaxed, open manner instantly took the edge off our nerves. Even though we barely understood a word, we felt welcome.

Since check-in at the hostel wasn't possible until the afternoon, we decided to walk to the promenade. The sun was high, the light harsh, and the heat shimmered off the asphalt. Barefoot, we sat down at the edge of the water, dipped our tired feet in, and enjoyed the moment of arrival.

We had finally made it. And then, of course, I missed the

sign. A sign with a crocodile on it. A man called out from the side:

*»There are crocodiles in there!«*

I only understood "crocodile", but that was enough. Instinctively, I jumped up, let out a startled scream, and took two quick steps back, while Nati was practically doubled over with laughter.

Welcome to Australia, the country where everything tries to kill you. But thankfully, everything turned out fine. No crocodiles, no more panic. Just two exhausted backpackers slowly beginning to realise: this is our life now. From today on, the adventure begins. And this was only the beginning.

Eventually, the time came, and we were finally allowed to check into our hostel room. Another small milestone ticked off our list. I had booked the stay months in advance, just to make sure we had a roof over our heads for at least the first week or two – better safe than sorry. Anything else would have completely overwhelmed us.

Check-in? A mix of improvisation and internal hysterics. There we were, with our massive backpacks, completely exhausted and absolutely overwhelmed, and now we were supposed to communicate in English. I looked at the woman at reception, nodded with confident German determination and simply said:

*»Check-in?«*

That was all I could manage at that moment. She asked us a few questions, talked a lot, pointed at things on the screen, and we just kept nodding and repeating,

*»Okay. Yes. Okay.«*

We had absolutely no idea what she had just explained to us. It was all too much – too fast, too unclear, too Australian. I mean, how could we have known better?

Back in school we had English classes, technically, but they were anything but motivating. Our teacher was a strict, overly rigid woman with questionable methods. She ran through her lessons with military precision, probably planned down to the minute the night before just so she could later pat herself on the back. You couldn't say a single wrong word, otherwise she'd kick you out. She seemed to actively look for reasons to tell someone off. And once she had it in for you, that was it.

In my case, I had already lost twice. My brother had been in her class years before me, and let's just say their past was… tense. The moment she heard my last name, it was clear she threw me into the same category. For her, I was just "the little Janko sister," and basically unwelcome from day one. So the chances of actually learning anything? Close to zero. Real English skills? A gamble. What we got was a mix of pressure, frustration, and the constant effort to make it through the class without becoming a target. Nati and I never really learned it.

But now here we were – in Australia. And if there was one place where you absolutely had to learn English, it was here. And you know what? Today, in 2025, I speak fluent English. Sometimes I can hardly believe it myself. But it really happened! Because back then, we were brave. We communicated with our hands and feet, armed with Google Translate, and never stopped learning.

After all the confusion, the struggle to understand the receptionist, and our desperate attempts to revive our rusty school English from the back of our brains, the friendly woman finally showed us our room, with a smile and an energetic:

*»Follow me, girls!«*

she led the way, and we shuffled behind her, still half jet-lagged, but as excited as two little kids heading off to their first night at camp. When she swung open the door and presented us the room with a dramatic gesture, we knew instantly: this was going to be… interesting.

Our first hostel room — a six-bed female dorm, and it was absolute chaos. Clothes were scattered across every bed, half-open suitcases blocked the narrow walkways, a bra was draped over the door handle like it belonged there, and from one corner came a snore that sounded like an exhausted bear in hibernation. Welcome to real hostel life.

And then: our first shower. Five narrow cubicles, one flimsy curtain each, no shelves for shampoo, no hooks for clothes. The floor was damp, the air sticky, and yet: the warm water finally running over our bodies after that never-ending journey felt like a hug. Honestly, it was the best moment of the day.

After a rather restless night, where our bodies seemed to jolt awake every two hours, we eventually woke up as if on autopilot. Our internal clocks were completely out of sync. Was it early morning? Or already midday? Didn't matter. It was light outside, that was good enough for orientation. We sat up and looked around: clothes were still scattered everywhere, a pair of pants hung over the reading lamp, my shoes had mysteriously found their way under a stranger's bed. Welcome to our very first real backpacker morning.

Before we could even think about tackling the chaos, our stomachs growled. Breakfast was calling. So we dragged ourselves, tired and disoriented, into the common room, still completely out of rhythm, but determined to find something, anything, to eat.

No more German breakfasts. No fresh bread rolls, no cheese, no lovingly set table with tiny jars of jam and Nutella. Instead: toast. Eggs. Baked beans. And, of course, Vegemite. That legendary Aussie spread that tastes like someone smeared salty broth on a kitchen sponge. Australians love it. We… not so much. But we gave it a brave try, pulled funny faces, laughed, and agreed that we probably wouldn't do that again anytime soon.

Back in our room, it finally started to sink in: we were backpackers now. And backpackers save wherever they can, even when it comes to laundry. Which meant: washing things by hand. Like proper backpackers do. In a tiny sink, with way too much detergent, zero patience, and absolutely no idea what we were doing. Our hands looked like raisins after just ten minutes, the clothesline outside our room was more symbolic than stable, and the wind blew our socks right across the courtyard.

After our freshly washed laundry had steamed away in the tropical sun for a while, we headed straight into town. It was time to tick off the first items on our to-do list: applying for a tax file number, opening a bank account, getting an Australian phone number. Of course, we didn't manage all of that at once, but step by step, it started to feel like we were actually arriving.

Our second day in Australia. The sun was shining as if it wanted to welcome us personally. Nati and I strolled along the Cairns Esplanade, feeling the warmth on our skin and trying to soak in this new continent. It still felt surreal.

We explored the town, wandered through supermarkets like Coles and Woolworths, marvelling at the shelves as if we were in a museum, laughing at things that were completely foreign to us. Shelves full of Vegemite. Weet-Bix, Lamingtons, crumpets, and chips with chicken salt flavour.

At some point, we sat down in the shade and asked ourselves the big question:

»*Should we maybe start looking for a car?*«

The idea came quickly and instantly felt right. So, we started searching on Facebook Marketplace, Gumtree, and with the help of other backpackers at the hostel.

One thing was clear: buying a car in Australia is a science in itself. You need a bit of luck, and a good dose of caution. A lot of backpackers try to sell their vehicles at the last minute, just before flying home, with registrations about to expire or gearboxes barely hanging on after thousands of kilometres on the road. Luckily, there was this one German backpacker at our hostel who helped us out. Our English was still pretty… terrible. She translated for us, asked all the right questions, and probably saved us from ending up with two rolling disasters.

The first two inspections? Let's just say they were underwhelming. One car rattled the moment it started, the other smelled like damp carpet. Both probably wouldn't have made it to the next petrol station.

But then came the third viewing. Two German girls, just like us. They had just finished their trip around Australia and were selling their Nissan Pathfinder. The moment we saw it, we just knew: this was our car. It was spacious, well looked after, perfectly built out, and gleaming gold in the sun.

Goldi. That's what we called him, even before we'd officially bought him.

The conversation was in German, the trust was there, and the payment? A breeze. We transferred the money straight from our German bank account to theirs — no fee drama, no language barriers. Easy.

We sat in the afternoon sun on the carpark, feeling the warmth on our skin as we looked over at Goldi – our shiny new adventure on four wheels. But it wasn't just a car. Not to us. It was already more than that. A home on wheels. A promise. A little slice of freedom with four tyres and golden paint that sparkled in the sun like pure happiness.

Somewhere between sunbeams, red dust and that quiet but steadily growing anticipation, it began to take shape – our first road trip plan. Not written down yet, no fixed route or destination, but it was already alive in our minds. And in the midst of it all, a thought quietly nestled its way in – the Outback. The vast nothingness. The red centre of Australia. We didn't know when we'd go, or how we'd even manage it, but the feeling was there. That tingle. That little spark telling us: we want to go where hardly anyone goes. Into the heart of the country.

Maybe it was just a fleeting idea, born somewhere between sunset and supermarket, but it wouldn't let us go.

∫⌒

We made a list. A long one. And with every item, we planned a little more of our adventure. Goldi was fuelled up – not just with petrol, but with all our dreams.

Oil level, water, tyre pressure, it all had to be checked. Or better said: someone from the hostel helped us out while we stood by with serious expressions, nodding thoughtfully as if we knew exactly what we were doing. Of course we had no clue. But that was okay. That's what friendly hostel people were for.

Then came the next big step: supplies. We pushed our trolley through the aisles like two teenagers grocery shopping for the first time without their parents. Snacks, pasta, muesli bars, cans in all shapes and colours, and water. Lots of water. Bottle after bottle. And of course, a small red petrol canister with five litres inside, our personal emergency backup plan. At the time, we thought that was incredibly clever. How much we'd come to regret that decision later on… we had no idea. A gas cooker was also a must – plus gas bottles. Some cutlery, two plates, a can opener. Everything two girls might need to avoid starving in the middle of nowhere. But my personal pride and joy – my own heartfelt contribution to the setup, was the pillows. So many pillows. I completely lost myself in Kmart. Every colour, every pattern, every soft, fluffy bit of fabric felt like a piece of home I just had to take with me. Two pillows? Not enough. Three? A joke. By the end, it looked like I was planning to take an entire lounge suite. Nati was shocked. Even after just a few days, my pillows were already in the way — while sleeping, while packing, while cooking. Actually… always.

*»Anne, this is a car, not a Pinterest room!«*

Nati laughed as she fought her way through the soft chaos for the fifth time. But what can I say? As long as it looked nice and I was happy. Even if no one else ever needed, or wanted, those pillows.

We laughed a lot during those early days. About ourselves, about my completely over-the-top pillow obsession that got in the way no matter what we were doing, and about that little red jerry can that stood bravely in the corner as if it might one day save our asses.

We laughed about our slightly chaotic plans — ones that sounded like we knew what we were doing, even though, truth be told, we didn't even really know where we were headed. All we knew was: we wanted to go. Out there. Somewhere that smelled like freedom and where the roads were covered in dust.

When we finally packed everything in, Goldi was filled to the roof — with food, gear, pillow chaos, and a healthy dose of delusion. We looked at each other and exchanged a glance that said it all. No big words. Just a shared thought:

*»Right then… what could possibly go wrong?«*

# CHAPTER FOUR
OUTBACK

The tank was full. The car packed. The sun was already blazing early in the morning as we stepped out of our hostel room for the last time. It was hot, but it felt right. We no longer wore our backpacks like clueless tourists, we wore them like people who knew this was the real deal now. We took one last look at the hostel, the place where our beautiful chaos had all begun, then climbed into our Nissan Pathfinder. A quiet click, the engine started, windows down, and off we went.

Our first destination? No idea. Well, sort of, but only vaguely. We weren't heading to the busy East Coast like everyone else. Not to Byron Bay or Sydney, where the waves call and the cafés are always full. No, our road would lead us right into the heart of Australia – to the centre, where the land is raw, silent, and still deeply untouched. Our goal:

Uluru, more commonly known as Ayers Rock. But "Uluru" is the original name given by the Pitjantjatjara people, the traditional custodians of this land, and it had existed long before any European settlers set foot here.

From Cairns, we drove straight into the Outback — along scorching highways, past rusty old roadhouses and tiny settlements you could miss if you blinked.

The route? A proper challenge, not just mentally, but in every practical sense too. Some petrol stations were over 300 kilometres apart. We were convinced we were well prepared. Or, to be more honest: we simply hoped we were.

The roads grew emptier with every hour. The landscape wilder. The air drier, and our minds clearer. We weren't in civilisation anymore, we were in the middle of it all. You can drive for hours without seeing a single house. No phone signal. No people. Just you, your car, and the endless horizon that never seems to get closer. On either side: red dirt. Shrubs, eucalyptus trees, towering termite mounds, and a kind of silence so deep it almost buzzes, simply because we're no longer used to it. But it was beautiful. Breathtaking. You feel small, but free.

We rolled the windows down, let the warm wind rush in and sang our hearts out to whatever came through the Bluetooth speaker. And then, suddenly, right there on the highway: my first kangaroo. Dead. Just lying there. Dried out, dishevelled, almost surreal.

Later, we'd pass dead cows, wallabies, emus... Australia isn't just wild, it's brutally honest. But somewhere between all those confronting sights, there were moments that felt almost magical. The sky began to shift into shades of pomegranate and soft peach, like someone had brushed a pastel painting across the horizon. The colours were gentle, warm, and they signalled the end of a day that had felt longer than usual. The further we drove, the more the world behind us faded away. The cities, the traffic, the phone signal, it was as if the world had decided to leave us be.

In front of us lay only the road. Dusty, shimmering road. And above it, that endless sky. The bush barely changed, and yet there was so much to see. A flock of black cockatoos lifted off right in front of us. A massive eagle circled above the road, almost as if welcoming us. Dry grass rustled in the wind, and twisted old trees cast long shadows. The air smelled of heat, of dirt, eucalyptus and dust. Our engine hummed quietly as we clocked up the kilometres. Everything seemed slower out here. Our thoughts. Our movements. Even the way we breathed.

And then there was that horizon — so vast, you weren't sure it would ever come closer. That wide open space was overwhelming. A little intimidating. But more than anything: freeing.

At some point, with the sun already low on the horizon, we decided it was time to find a place to sleep. We came across a free campsite, somewhere in the middle of nowhere. No lights, no showers, no phone reception. Luckily, we'd had a long hot shower back at the hostel that morning, otherwise things could've gotten a bit rough on our very first night.

There was just us, our car, and the night, wrapping itself around us like a soft, protective blanket. But this night was unlike any I'd ever experienced. When we stepped out of the car and looked up at the sky, we both froze for a moment. There wasn't a single artificial light, no noise, no distractions. Just darkness, and millions of stars. So many, it looked like the entire sky was on fire. I had never seen anything like it. So clear, so vast, so close. It felt like someone had set up a planetarium right above us, only without a ceiling in the way. Every shooting star, every little flicker in the sky felt within reach. You could follow the Milky Way with your bare eyes, stretching across the heavens like a glowing ribbon. I just stood there, mouth open, unable to take it all in.

We fell asleep early — exhausted, but completely at peace.

The next morning, we woke up in the middle of the Outback. Not a sound, except for the birds slowly starting to stir.

The sun was already blazing overhead, and the air was dry and shimmering with heat. A completely different climate to Cairns. No more tropical humidity, just dry heat and that unrelenting sun that hangs over this continent almost every day of the year. Nati and I pulled out our little camping table, laid out a few slices of toast and some Nutella. It was nothing fancy, and didn't think much of it.

We just wanted to pop over to the drop toilet for a minute. But when we returned five minutes later, everything was gone. Not stolen by people—no, by birds. The cheekiest, hungriest, most shameless feathered thieves Australia has to offer. They'd snatched our toast, torn open the wrappers, and left the rest scattered across the ground like a crime scene. We stood there, laughing and swearing all at once. Of course, how could we forget that out here, the animals are just as desperate for food as we are for breakfast? In this dry, sunburnt land, every scrap counts. Especially if two blondes leave it unattended.

We learned quickly: in Australia, you don't leave anything out. Not even for five minutes.

Eventually, somewhere between two termite mounds and yet another endless stretch of road, our stomachs started rumbling again. And as it goes when you've got nothing around, you get creative. I was in the passenger seat, Nati was driving, and I decided it was time for lunch—on the move.

Behind us, somewhere between the gas cooker, water jugs and piles of blankets, sat our open fruit and veggie basket. And by "open," I mean an absolute mess. Nothing sorted, everything rolling around freely. By the end of each day it was like an Easter egg hunt just to find a stray cucumber or apple lodged between the mattress and the car door. I reached back blindly, pulled out our wooden chopping board, which, as always, was annoyingly in the way, and started slicing tomatoes and cucumbers on my lap. My hands looked like I'd wrestled a greenhouse. Tomato juice everywhere, cucumber water dripping, and no napkins in sight. But hey, Nati was getting fed. While driving.

I held out the slices like tiny canapés, and she accepted them gratefully. Because, and I say this with love, Nati when she's hungry is… let's call it a challenge. A cross between a diva, a chaos queen, and a slightly deranged gremlin. But if I'm being honest, I'm not much better.

At some point, I chucked the leftovers out the window, thinking they'd disappear into the nothingness. They didn't. The tomato juice splattered across the side of the car, cucumber water trickled down the glass, and the wind did the rest. The whole car ended up smelling like a compost heap. Nati looked at me, speechless at first, and then we both burst out laughing. The kind of laughter that gives you cramps and makes your stomach hurt. Not a romantic "We'll never forget this" kind of moment. More like:

*»What the hell are we actually doing here?«*

After hours of shimmering asphalt, parched throats and a bum that was starting to feel like cardboard, the saving grace finally appeared: Fuel.

We'd made it to Croydon. Or at least to what called itself that. Maybe five houses, a few crooked verandas, and a petrol station that looked like something out of an old Western film. No supermarket, no café, not a single soul in sight – just heat, dust, and that odd feeling that time ticks a little differently out here. The pump was slightly rusted, and the humming fridge made a sound like it was breathing its last as we opened it. And yet, this place had charm, in a weird way. Not the kind of charm that makes you think,

*»Yeah, I could grow old here«* more like:
*»Once is enough.«*

We got out, stretched, and shuffled towards the counter in our thongs like two dehydrated zombies. Filled up the tank, grabbed an ice-cold Coke, and took a deep breath. I looked around and wondered what it must be like to live here – in this stillness, this vastness, this isolation. So far from all the hustle I never liked anyway. Crowds have never been my thing. Even with thirty people in one place, I start asking myself, *"Is this really necessary?"* I've always had a soft spot for solitude, for wide open space, for room to breathe. If I could truly choose, my home would be somewhere in the countryside. No neighbours in sight, maybe just a few horses at the gate. Ideally, there'd be green meadows, a waterfall in the backyard (why not?), mountains on the horizon, the ocean around the corner and a lake for swimming right behind the house. A little farm – not for slaughter, just for cuddles. Mornings greeting the cows, afternoons scratching goats behind the ears, and evenings with a cup of tea on the veranda, watching the sunset. That would be my dream. Alright, maybe a bit cheesy,but absolutely true.

Croydon definitely wasn't it. But still, it was fascinating to see it. To experience how people live out here, far from supermarkets, from 5G reception, from high-rises and coffee chains. They seemed content. They lived slowly. Maybe happiness really does look different for everyone. For me, it was right there in that moment, somewhere between a can of Coke, dusty shoes, and the thought of a home that didn't exist yet, but was already crystal clear in my mind.

We had over six hours of driving ahead of us before reaching the next town. Our next destination: Mount Isa. Even just the name sounded like an oasis. We pictured ourselves pushing air-conditioned shopping trolleys through endless aisles in search of bananas, rice cakes, and maybe— just maybe, a proper shower.

The road there seemed to stretch on forever. Once again, kilometre after kilometre of red sand, shimmering air, and that overwhelming sense of nothingness as far as the eye could see. The bitumen glistened in the heat like liquid metal, while the dust slowly settled on our windscreen, as if it wanted to come along for the ride. Every two hours, we swapped drivers. The kind of focus required out here brought a very particular kind of fatigue.

You stare straight ahead, endlessly straight ahead, and eventually wonder if anything's actually moving at all, besides your own thoughts.

⌒

Our mission was clear: Mount Isa. A town that felt like the promised land, full of supplies, civilisation, and chilled water stacked neatly in real shelves.

We needed to refuel. Not just Goldi, but ourselves. Petrol, water, food, a few gas canisters for cooking, anything to keep us alive in this unforgiving yet mesmerising vastness.

Because as romantic as an Outback road trip might sound, at some point you'll inevitably ask yourself the same question:

*»So… what the hell are we eating tonight?«*

And here comes my confession: Nati and I, we love cooking— at home. In actual kitchens. With stovetops, ovens, herbs, and space. We'd be the first to whip up a creative meal from leftovers, glass of red in hand, spices at our fingertips. But out there, with a wobbly gas cooker, no fridge, no running water, and a knife that resembled a blunt butter spreader from a preschool, our passion for cooking turned into more of a survival tactic.

Our signature dish? Fried potatoes with red capsicum. Every. Single. Night. It was easy, filling, and somehow… ritualistic. But the real star of our Outback dinners—the absolute highlight, was hands down the 'Cream Cheese & Chive' Dip from Woolworths. To this day, I have no idea why it tasted so good. Maybe because it added something beyond just salt and spuds. Or maybe because, once you let go of everything else, you start to truly appreciate the small things.

We'd sit there in the evenings, on our camping chairs, the car serving as a crooked backrest, our feet in the dust, a sky full of stars above us—the kind of sky you only see far away from city lights, and eat.

With every bite of potato-capsicum-mush and every scoop of dip, we realised: this was something special. Not the food. Not the comfort. But this moment. This simple, honest, imperfect life. You relearn how to marvel, at cold cans of Coke, foldable forks, and a humble chive-flavoured dip. Even though we were slowly getting sick of fried potatoes, it was still special every time to eat under the open sky, in the middle of nowhere, with dusty shoes and tired eyes. It wasn't the big things that mattered, it was the small ones: a warm meal, a familiar flavour, a moment of peace. You quickly learn that with very little, you can still have quite a lot.

When we finally arrived in Mount Isa, it almost felt unreal. After all those days in the middle of nowhere, it was nearly a culture shock to suddenly see more than three buildings at once. Petrol stations. Supermarkets. People. But something else struck us too: Mount Isa is home to many Aboriginal peoples – the First Nations of this continent.

We saw groups gathered around the town, at bus stops, in parks. Although we were only there to do some grocery shopping, there was a certain tension in the air. Not hostile, more cautious, reserved. Maybe it was because we were new here. But maybe it was also because we knew the history.

The relationship between European settlers and the First Nations peoples is not a proud one.

When the British colonised Australia in the 18th century, they declared it "Terra Nullius" – "nobody's land". In doing so, they ignored the fact that Aboriginal peoples had lived on this continent for over 60,000 years. What followed was a period of displacement, violence, dispossession, and cultural erasure. Many people lost their homes, their families, their languages. To this day, many Indigenous communities still carry the weight of that injustice: poverty, racism, exclusion. It's not their fault. It's our shared history, and one that remains far from reconciled.

So there we stood, two young travellers, tired, hungry, and a little overwhelmed, knowing one thing for sure: we were guests in this country, and that's something you should never forget.

After we'd explored Mount Isa a little and ticked everything off our to-do list, we hit the road again. We were over the noise and bustle of town. All we wanted was to be back in the wide open, somewhere we could fall asleep to the sound of crickets and feel the warm dust under our feet. Our destination: another free campsite.

As soon as we arrived, we unpacked our gas cooker setup like pros, grabbed our favourite veggies and – almost ceremoniously, opened a fresh tub of our sacred dip. Potatoes, capsicum, cream cheese & chives. A dish that would never make it onto a restaurant menu, but to us, it was gold.

We worked like clockwork – Nati on the cooker, me beside her with the chopping knife, and somewhere on the edge of the boot, wedged between the water canister and the food box, I chopped like there was no tomorrow. It was hot, dusty, and we were starving. When everything finally started sizzling and the smell filled the air, we sat side by side, waiting for that first bite, and every time we thought:

*»How can something this simple taste so bloody good?«*

And then came that moment again, the one that made everything else fade. Night slowly fell, and with it, the sky. Each night it seemed clearer. Deeper. Quieter. More magical. I honestly don't know how to put it into words… but I'd never seen that many stars in my life. Not on postcards. Not in a planetarium. But there, with my own eyes.

The moon was upside down! No joke. No exaggeration. It looked completely different in Australia than it did back home in Germany. Not just slightly off – completely flipped. I stared up at it and thought, Hang on a sec… that's not how it usually looks, is it? And sure enough: in the Southern Hemisphere, the moon appears upside down compared to how we see it in the Northern Hemisphere. It's all about the perspective – you're literally looking at it from the other side of the planet. What we call "up" in Europe becomes "down" in Australia. A small detail, sure. But one that reminds you that you really are on the other side of the world.

The next morning, we set off to complete the stretch to Uluru. There were still hundreds of kilometres ahead, but we felt it in our bones, that the hardest part was behind us.

Our next major milestone was Alice Springs, the heart of Australia. The landscape began to shift. It became more hilly, with denser bushland. No longer that same endless flatness, but somehow… more alive. And along the way, we stopped at a place you simply can't skip when travelling through the Red Centre: Karlu Karlu, also known as the Devil's Marbles.

Imagine being in the middle of the desert, surrounded by dry earth, scraggly bushes, endless road, and suddenly, giant rocks appear. Not just any boulders, but perfectly round, egg-shaped stone giants that look like someone deliberately placed them there.

After visiting Karlu Karlu, we drove another four hours or so until we reached Alice Springs. Surprisingly, the drive was pleasant. After all the isolated dirt roads, dusty rest stops, and endless horizons, it felt strangely surreal to be back on proper roads again. As we rolled into Alice Springs, a large rust-red sign greeted us:

*»Welcome to Alice Springs«*

The sign stood slightly elevated on a small hill. I climbed up, laughing, with my cowboy hat on and looked out over the vast nothingness beyond, an endless stretch of red earth, scattered bushes, and a horizon that just wouldn't quit. It felt a bit like a movie scene, somewhere between the Wild West and the romanticised version of the Australian outback.

Alice Springs took us by surprise. After days in the middle of nowhere, the town felt almost bustling: petrol stations, cafés, proper supermarkets, people actually walking along pavements. Nati and I wandered the streets, browsed a few small shops, sipped cold Coke from a can, and enjoyed this little dose of civilisation that felt like a reward, not spectacular, but exactly what we needed.

If you feel like it, you can even explore some nature here. Alice Springs is surrounded by stunning mountain ranges, gorges, and walking tracks. But for us, in that moment, it was enough to simply have a shower again, buy some fresh groceries, and enjoy the feeling of not sitting in the car for a day.

That evening, we found a spot to sleep, got cosy in the car, and fell asleep early. We knew: the next day, another long stretch of road lay ahead.

We left Alice Springs early in the morning and set off towards Kings Canyon — about four hours of driving lay ahead of us. The road to the canyon was, to put it mildly, a disaster. At some point, the sealed road just stopped, asphalt turned to gravel, and gravel turned to corrugated dirt tracks. Our car groaned at every bump, and we groaned with it. The plan was a two-hour drive. We ended up taking four. When we finally arrived at the car park, we were — once again, completely unprepared. No sunscreen, no emergency knife, one single bottle of water for two people, no signal, no reception.

Here's a little survival tip for the middle of nowhere: get Telstra. In the Outback, Vodafone is basically just decoration — reception? Not a chance. But honestly, reception was the last thing on our minds at that moment. Our focus was somewhere else entirely: Nati and I thought we'd just walk up, snap a few pretty photos, and be back at the car within two hours. What we didn't realise: the official sign said the hike would take three hours, and it ended up being six. Six hours. One bottle of water. Not a shred of shade. As dusk slowly settled in, we followed the small trail markers that were supposed to lead us back down — back to the car park, back to the car, back to safety.

But as it often goes when you think you're a bit of an adventurer, a bit of an Instagram star, and a bit invincible: we took photos. Loads of them! But eventually, we stood there with no idea where the path actually continued. No torch, both phones nearly dead, no power bank, and no emergency gear. For the first time on this trip, we felt genuine fear.

The sun was already low, the track ahead had vanished, and surrounded by those red cliffs, everything suddenly looked the same. My phone still had a few percent left, just enough for one final message.

Almost frantically, I typed to my mum:

*»Hey, just in case. We're somewhere at Kings Canyon and can't find the way back right now.«*.

I hit send without thinking too much. She was, let's put it diplomatically – not thrilled. Understandably so.

It was a strange feeling, knowing that we were completely on our own. No roads. No people. No signal. Just us, the confusing terrain, and that sinking feeling in our stomachs that was only growing.

While we desperately tried to find the way down, a massive kangaroo suddenly jumped out of nowhere right in front of us. We nearly died of fright. So close, so unexpected. It made our hearts stop for a second, and then we couldn't help but laugh. It was just all too much. The heat, the panic, the disorientation, and now a kangaroo with jump-scare level ten.

No other hikers in sight. No help. No reception. And then, glinting silver in the rock, we spotted something: an emergency box. With a satellite phone, and believe it or not – a sealed bottle of water. Officially only for emergencies. For us? Definitely an emergency. We drank from it, almost reverently, like it was sacred. It was the moment we knew: we'd been incredibly lucky.

Eventually, we finally found a staircase, winding its way down in switchbacks. Every step felt like a small promise: Almost there.

About two hours later, we were finally back at the car park and felt a huge wave of relief wash over us as our car came into view.

We found a free campsite nearby and drove straight there. The only thing we could think about was our bed – we snuggled up in all our pillows and blankets right away. We were completely wrecked, briefly talked about everything that had happened, and how things could've ended differently. That's when it really hit both of us just how lucky we'd been.

There are stories of tourists – even Aussies themselves, who've gotten lost in the Outback, underestimated the heat, or failed to find their way back.

I remembered the film Outback, a survival thriller based on a true story. An American couple gets lost in the Australian bush after their GPS fails, and they're pushed to their limits by the relentless nature. No reception, barely any water, dangerous animals, and decisions that mean the difference between life and death.

The film shows just how quickly an adventure can turn into a nightmare. Definitely worth watching, especially for anyone who thinks Australia is all red rocks and cute kangaroos.

We thought about how quickly our own day could've taken a different turn. We promised ourselves we'd be better prepared, less careless. But also: deeply grateful. Grateful for every step we were still able to take. For every night under that breathtaking starry sky. For every adventure that changes us.

# CHAPTER FIVE
## ULURU

After nearly two weeks on the road – over 2,500 kilometres across the Outback, past red dirt tracks, scorching heat, lonely petrol stations, quiet moments, and nights under millions of stars – the time had finally come. We were on the last stretch of our journey to Uluru.

That morning, we left Alice Springs early. The sun was still low in the sky as we rolled off again in our trusty car. Ahead of us lay another three and a half hours of driving. The landscape felt familiar – flat, vast, quiet. And yet, on this day, everything felt different. We knew: this was it, the big one. The road stretched out like a ribbon through the endless plain. And then, at some point, we saw it. At first, it was just a dark smudge on the horizon. A shape in the distance. But it grew bigger, clearer, more dominant, until there was no doubt left: that was it. Uluru. Rising out of the middle of nowhere. A massive, solitary red rock. No other hills, no mountains, nothing surrounding it. Just one rock. The largest freestanding monolith in the world. Standing 348 metres tall and spanning over nine kilometres around its base. It doesn't try to be spectacular – it simply is. Its colour shifts with the light, from dusty orange to deep crimson.

In the moment we first saw it, it almost looked like it was glowing. We'd been working our way towards it for two full weeks. And now, there it was. We didn't say a word. Our eyes were fixed on the window. For a moment, we forgot the heat, the dust, the exhaustion, and just stared in awe.

What many people don't realise, and what continues to surprise me, is how little some travellers actually know about Uluru. It's like travelling to China and asking,

»*What's the Great Wall again?*«

Honestly, it feels like a bit of a culture shock every time. When we finally arrived at Uluru, we could sense just how much meaning and expectation surrounds this place – not just for us, but for an entire country, for an entire people. Uluru isn't just some big rock in the desert. It's deeply rooted in the culture and history of the Anangu, the Pitjantjatjara and Yankunytjatjara peoples who have lived in connection with this land for thousands of years. Its shape, its surface, even the shadows it casts tell stories – the Tjukurpa, ancient Dreamtime stories that speak of creation and meaning. To outsiders, that might sound a little abstract. But when you're standing in front of it, you understand: this is not just a rock.

We parked the car, walked a few steps closer, and had to tilt our heads back just to take it all in. Uluru felt like something from another world – raw, red, immense. Not a place that screams for attention, but one that simply exists, powerful and still.

The air was warm, filled with the scent of sand and dry grass. There were no buildings, no noise, nothing but the wind. And that's what made it so special. The very fact that this rock has stood here for around 550 million years is humbling. It's survived geological ages, climate shifts, entire cultures – and it's still here. Towering. Unmissable. Unchanged.

We set off on the roughly ten-kilometre base walk. The thermometer showed a pleasant 28°C, and a light breeze softened the midday sun just enough.

This time, we were well prepared – plenty of water, sunscreen, and sturdy shoes. But it quickly became clear: this wasn't just a casual stroll. The path ran over hot, sandy ground, often without the slightest hint of shade. Every step demanded focus and endurance. And then there were the flies. Millions of them. Buzzing into our noses, ears, eyes – literally everywhere. It's hard to describe unless you've experienced it yourself. They hovered around like tiny, annoying shadows, making you momentarily forget that you were supposed to be marvelling at a natural wonder. It was maddening, and eventually, kind of funny.

Still, with every step, a new view unfolded before us: sharp outlines carved into the steep, towering rock walls, deep dark crevices, and glowing shades of red and ochre that lit up in the sunlight.

About halfway along, we spotted a small wooden bench. Nati sat down, and I simply flopped across her legs. My head heavy, my body exhausted. It was one of those silent pauses where everything just… stops for a moment. And then, out of nowhere, a little lizard crawled towards us. Slowly, completely unbothered, it settled into the shade beneath the bench and just stayed there. Almost as if it, too, needed a break. It remained with us until we got back up and continued walking – a quiet companion with dry skin and perfect Outback vibes.

Shortly after, as we rounded a gentle bend, we saw a woman from the Aboriginal community sitting on a rocky ledge. She was calm, quiet, and looked as though she belonged entirely to that place. She gazed towards Uluru and was explaining to a small group of tourists what this place meant. She didn't sound like she was giving a lecture, more like someone sharing a story that had been passed down for generations.

We sat down, listened quietly, didn't say a word. Even if we didn't catch every single thing, one thing was clear straight away: this place meant everything to her. The way she spoke – calm, steady, full of depth, made it obvious how much knowledge and connection lived in her words.

---

The final few kilometres really tested us. Our legs were heavy, the sun was blazing, and the flies? Oh, they'd fully committed to joining us for the rest of the journey. But our phones? Packed. Completely maxed out. Over a thousand new pictures – red dirt, rock shapes, shadows, sky, and us in every possible angle. And still, somehow, it felt like none of them truly showed what it felt like to be there. It had been one of those stunning, unforgettable days.

When the sun started to sink behind Uluru, it was like a silent grand finale. The rock turned this deep, glowing orange, almost as if it were lighting up just to say goodbye. We stood there, completely quiet, and just knew: this moment would stay with us forever.

That night, we treated ourselves to a proper campground – yep, a paid one this time. But honestly, we were glad. There were hot showers, a little Outback kitchen, and for the first time in what felt like ages, it all felt a tiny bit… civilised again.

We had treated ourselves to a few groceries the day before in Alice Springs, including lamb for dinner. A little highlight after days of pan-fried potatoes with capsicum and cream cheese & chive dip.

We cooked, plated everything in the tiny kitchen, then sat outside, across from each other – tired but happy. While we sat at the wooden bench of the open campground kitchen, hungry but content, we scrolled through the day's photos. The sky was already dark, and the heat of the day had given way to the dry coolness of an Outback evening. It was quiet, almost too quiet.

Then Nati suddenly said with a tense look:
»Anne..there's a dog off-leash… something's weird.«

I didn't even need to look. Just the tone of her voice was enough to know, that's not a dog. It was a dingo! He stood just a few metres away, eyes fixed on our lamb on the table

– motionless, focused. No barking, no twitching, just that one stare.

Quick side note: Dingoes are Australia's wild dogs. At first glance, they look like regular mutts – lean, sandy-coloured, with pointed ears and sharp eyes. But they're not pets. They live in the wild, hunt on their own, are shy but not harmless, especially when food is involved.

For a moment, everything went completely silent. We looked at each other. Didn't say a word. Then, simultaneously, we both looked at Goldi. Without saying a word, we jumped up – abruptly, panicked, and bolted. The dingo seized his moment. With one leap, he was on the table, snatched the meat like a pro, and vanished into the darkness. We flung Goldi's doors open, threw ourselves into the seats, and locked everything like we were in some bad horror movie. Inside: pounding hearts. Outside: silence. Then we looked at each other, and burst out laughing.

*»Well, there goes the lamb,«*

I muttered, wiping my forehead. Just another evening in the Outback. Simply unforgettable.

# CHAPTER SIX

BACK TO THE GREEN

It was time to head back. After all those days in the Outback – the heat, the dust, the red roads, we set off on the journey from Uluru back to Cairns. More than 2,400 kilometres lay ahead. Almost the exact same route as on the way there, just in reverse, with fewer breaks, fewer detours, and a whole lot more of that "let's just push through now" attitude. The big adventures were behind us – or so we thought.

We stopped here and there. A roadside rest area. A small town. Sometimes a sign that sounded promising. But our eyes were fixed ahead. On Cairns. Palm trees, rainforest, tropical air, and finally, the ocean again. We were excited. After so many days of red earth, we could hardly wait to see green again. That lush, wild, vibrant green of the northeast.

As always, I already had a thousand plans racing through my mind for what we could do there. Just a few more weeks – one, maybe two, in and around Cairns. It almost sounded like a holiday. Almost. Then honestly, even if we'd wanted to, there was no way to slow either of us down. As soon as we arrived somewhere, we were already thinking about the next place. Australia was simply too vast, too beautiful, too wild to just do nothing.

And yet, that one moment on the highway towards the coast, with the sun behind us and the GPS reading "1,800 km to Cairns", had something strangely comforting about it. The longest stretch was behind us. Soon we'd be breathing in tropical air again and starting our next chapter.

The drive dragged on. We were on the road for about a week — all the way across the continent, from the dry centre back to the lush, green northeast. Every day meant hours of sitting, driving, marvelling, pushing through. Even though we recognised many places from the way there, it somehow felt different. More familiar. Almost as if Australia wanted to show us everything once more before we finally reached the greenery. The temperatures grew milder. The deep red of the earth began to fade, and slowly the first trees started to look properly green again — not that dry bush green, but vibrant and alive. It felt as if someone had turned the colour dial back up.

Then suddenly, we were there: Cairns. A city that, for many, is just a starting point or a dot at the end of the map, but to us, it felt like arriving. Like a deep breath. Like salt on the skin and tropical air in the lungs. We were relieved. As much as we'd loved the Outback, it also felt good to not have to drive 600 kilometres every single day anymore.

We parked the car, got out, and it felt like the ground was still vibrating beneath our feet from all the hours on the road. But we had made it, and just like always when we arrived somewhere, it wasn't just peace we felt. There was also a new plan. Or rather: a thousand new ideas of what we could still do in Cairns.

Back in Cairns. Suddenly, everything felt familiar again. We checked into the same hostel where our Australian adventure had begun weeks before. Same reception area. Same smell of sunscreen, backpacks and wanderlust. Same squeaky bed frame, and yet it felt completely different now. It felt like home.

Nati and I finally had time not just to rush from one place to the next, but to actually arrive — to discover what Cairns had to offer. And it turned out, it had a lot.

One of the first things we booked was a 30-minute helicopter flight over the Great Barrier Reef. Extremely expensive. But worth every bloody cent. You can't imagine how vast, colourful, vibrant, and at the same time fragile this reef is until you see it from above. It looked like a living artwork in the turquoise-blue water. From up there, we saw huge manta rays gliding through the sea like creatures from another world. Between shimmering reflections dancing on the surface, we could spot dark, moving shadows – perhaps a school of fish, maybe a turtle. The reef's colours looked as if they had been painted on with a brush: bright turquoise, deep blue, and greenish patches that constantly shifted depending on the sunlight. From above, everything appeared peaceful, harmonious, and at the same time fragile, like a painting you instinctively don't want to touch.

A few days later, we went into the water on a guided snorkelling tour of the Great Barrier Reef. Just the idea of it felt like a dream.

*»I mean, snorkelling in the world's largest coral reef? Was this really my life or was I dreaming?«*

But as beautiful as it was, it also had its dark sides. Many of the corals were dead. You could see it with the naked eye – pale areas, broken structures. Some due to intense sun exposure, but many simply because tourists touch, walk on or break them – just for a photo. And yes, I'm someone who loves taking beautiful pictures, capturing moments, sharing memories. But we need to stop touching everything that fascinates us. Corals are living organisms – sensitive, slow-growing, vulnerable. One careless grab, a kick with a fin, and something that took decades to grow dies within minutes. The fact that so many people just whip out their selfie sticks, touch everything, and completely ignore what they're damaging – to be honest, it was shocking.

Then, right in the middle of this train of thought, we suddenly heard a loud scream coming from the water:

*»Shark! Shark! Shark!«*

I spun around instantly, and saw Nati staring at me through her completely fogged-up diving mask, as if she'd just seen how our trip was about to end in blood. And the best part? I, the one who's usually the dramatic one, stayed calm. I just said:

*»We're going to swim back to the boat calmly now. No sudden movements and we keep checking below us.«*

And that's exactly what we did. Around us, everyone started moving back to the boat, and no one really knew what was going on. The mood was tense, quiet, but not panicked. Every few seconds, we glanced into the water—down into the blue. But there was nothing. Once on board, they said it was a false alarm. Maybe a shadow. Maybe an overly excited sighting. Maybe someone who had just watched a few too many shark documentaries.

We were allowed back in the water. But let's just say, the carefree feeling was gone. You snorkel differently when you're suddenly aware that this isn't just a tropical playground. It's also home to creatures that are much bigger and far better adapted than we are.

Australia is beautiful. But also wild. The ocean doesn't belong to us. It never has, and it never will. Out there, different rules apply, different rhythms. It belongs to those who have lived in it for millions of years. Sharks, for example. You can't control it, can't predict it. If you go into the water, you know that, or at least you should. There's always a bit of risk. A moment of trust.

But that doesn't mean sharks are monsters. The fear we feel when we hear the word "shark" is often irrational, shaped more by Hollywood than by reality. The truth is: we are not on their menu. Shark attacks are incredibly rare, and yet we kill over 100 million sharks every year, mostly for nothing more than their fins. In comparison, only a handful of people die from shark encounters annually. We need sharks.

Desperately. They are apex predators, vital for maintaining the balance of marine ecosystems. Without enough sharks, fish populations explode or collapse, coral reefs suffer, and the entire food chain begins to unravel. The ocean loses its stability. And when the oceans lose balance, so do we — because everything is connected. Killing sharks out of fear isn't just cruel, it's dangerously shortsighted. Anyone who thinks the world would be safer without sharks has no idea what that would actually mean. A healthy ocean needs healthy shark populations. The problem isn't the sharks. It's our lack of understanding.

The wind blew through our hair as the boat glided calmly across the open sea. We sat at the back of the deck, legs stretched out, faces turned to the sun. Around us, the water whooshed by, seagulls circled above, and the glint of the waves sparkled like tiny lights moving in time with the ocean. I stared out into the endless blue, and suddenly a thought struck me:

*»What if I had never taken this step? What if I hadn't set off for Australia with Nati? Would I be sitting in the barracks' medical centre right now, filling out patient files, staring out the window and wondering if there was something more out there for me? Would I be dreaming of days like this, without ever having lived even one of them?«.*

Now I was here, in the middle of the Great Barrier Reef, the largest coral reef in the world—on a boat, in swimwear, hair sticky with saltwater, skin warm from the sun.

Then the crew brought lunch: egg salad sandwiches, carrot and cucumber sticks with hummus, salty vinegar chips, and for dessert, fresh mango and watermelon slices. Simple, but perfect after a long day in the water.

Back at the hostel, we treated ourselves to a hot shower, scrubbed the salt from our skin, and put on clean clothes. Then we sat next to each other on the bed—tired, but content, and let the day play back in our minds.

We watched the GoPro footage – colourful schools of fish, crystal-clear water, our carefree laughter in the background. Nothing grand, no spectacle. But those little things, they were what made it special. Like every night, we told each other everything again, even though we'd just lived it together.

We called our families, scrolled through our phones for a bit, and at some point, there was just silence. Just us, that comforting feeling of content exhaustion, and a day that we'd never forget.

# CHAPTER SEVEN

WATERFALLS & HIKING TRAILS

The time we spent in Cairns felt like a breath of fresh air. We had no set schedule, no route, no pressure—just us, our hostel bed, an open kitchen, and the endless possibilities of the tropical north.

We made the most of every day. We went out partying, met new people, spent hours sitting with other backpackers on wooden benches in the hostel's communal area, sharing stories, swapping itineraries, laughing at our language mishaps, and slowly realising: our English was getting better. Not perfect, but fluent enough. And that was all we really wanted.

Every day was different. Sometimes we planned spontaneous trips. Other times we just wandered aimlessly. But most of all, we craved nature.

We set out to explore the Atherton Tablelands—a region so

lush, so vibrant, and yet so peaceful that it made us forget we were still in the same country that only days ago had been all red sand and heat.

Our first stop: the Barron Falls. We stood on the viewing platform, leaning against the railing as we watched the water thunder down into the depths below. It was breathtaking, the sheer force, the roar, the fine mist hanging in the humid air. The sun was blazing, but up there it felt as if the air had grown heavier, thicker – almost like the jungle after a rainstorm. The spray rose and settled on our skin like a thin veil. The view into the gorge was mesmerising. You just couldn't look away.

A few days later, the tour took us to Millaa Millaa Falls, about 100 km southwest of Cairns. The area is known as the "Waterfall Circuit," and this particular waterfall stole the show. Surrounded by dense rainforest, the pool beneath glowed turquoise in the sun, and the curtain of water fell 18 metres into the valley, forming a backdrop straight out of a postcard.

We were with a German friend who was eager to show us this waterfall – she'd been there several times and laughed as she told us that actual shampoo commercials had been filmed there. And honestly, it made sense. The scene was so perfect, it almost felt unreal.

We splashed around in the clear water, took photos and giggled like kids as we tried to emerge gracefully from under the waterfall with our wet hair. Truth be told, by that point we were completely knackered.

Too many waterfalls in one day, too many impressions, too much awe. At some point your brain just gives up. All you want to do is sit, breathe, clear your head – and yet, you keep going. Not because you have to, but because some places simply won't wait for later.

∫ ⌒

A few days after our trip to Millaa Millaa Falls, we headed off to Wooroonooran National Park to see the famous Josephine Falls. Even the name sounded like something straight out of an adventure novel – and honestly, that's exactly how it felt.

Tucked away in the lush green of the tropical rainforest, water came rushing down a wide, sloping rock surface, so smooth that people actually tried to slide down it while standing. No joke. Some of them looked like pro surfers, others more like penguins on speed. We went for the safer method: sitting down. Which still hurt. A lot. But we laughed until we cried, kept sliding again and again, soaking wet and grinning like kids, somewhere between madness and waterpark fun, right in the heart of the rainforest.

It was a scorcher that day. Really hot. The sun pierced through the dense canopy, and the water was so ice-cold that it knocked the breath out of you the moment you jumped in, but that contrast made it absolutely perfect. Pure nature. Wild and unfiltered. And then came the part none of us will ever forget: our friend had the car key. In the side pocket of her swim shorts. Where it obviously shouldn't have been.

When she came out of the water and found the pocket empty, we just stared at each other. Everything went silent for a second. Then chaos broke loose.

We waded through the pool, dove under, felt every rock, cursed, laughed, froze. It felt like an underwater Easter egg hunt, with a lot more panic. After what felt like forever and at least fifty numb fingers, Nati finally found it: wedged between two flat rocks, glinting like a treasure from a pirate film. We screamed, squealed, hugged each other soaking wet. The drive home was saved. Our nerves... well, kind of too.

And just when we thought the day couldn't get any fuller, we met two German girls on our way back to the car – Alex and Vanessa. Also best friends, also travelling around Australia. We started chatting – first by the car, then at the boot, then somehow for way longer than expected. Sometimes you just click instantly. Same energy. Same humour. Same curiosity for life.

Back then, we had no idea that Alex would reappear at the end of my journey, in a completely different place, and that this encounter would blossom into a special friendship that would stay with me for a long time to come. But between now and then lay many more months and countless stories.

One of the most breathtaking places on our trip was Windin Falls. Not many people know about it, yet it's easily one of the most spectacular waterfalls in the tropical north. We had only heard about it a few days earlier and spontaneously decided to take the detour. The hike to get there? Often underestimated. Around 5.5 kilometres each way, so roughly 11 kilometres return, in over 30-degree heat, with barely any shade and a steady incline the whole time. Technically it wasn't a difficult trail, but the heat made it exhausting. Definitely doable for inexperienced hikers if you start early, take your time, and bring plenty of water.

We were prepared, and still, we arrived at the top sweaty and out of breath. But every single drop of sweat was worth it. Because suddenly, we were there — standing at the edge of this massive waterfall. In front of us lay a natural infinity pool, framed by rocks and crystal-clear water. Just beyond that: a sheer drop, and beyond that: endless wilderness. So green, so vast, so untouched. No houses, no roads, no sounds except for the roar of the waterfall and the wind sweeping through the valley. We carefully climbed onto the rocks and sat down to eat our lunch right by the water, at a safe distance from the edge, of course. I don't know if I've ever stared at a landscape with such fascination.

Nati scrambled up onto a slightly higher rock to take a photo of me as I lay in the water. I looked straight over the edge of the pool, and it felt like the edge of the world. The view was just absurdly beautiful. Like something out of a film. A green mosaic of forests, hills, and sky stretching all the way to the horizon. I could've sat there for hours. Still, the thought of the drop below made me a little uneasy.

The rocks were slippery, the water constantly moving — I was incredibly cautious. Maybe even a bit too much. But I couldn't help it. I've always been the kind of person who takes two steps back when it gets steep. Nati was braver, but even she watched every step.

Looking back, it was one of those days that sticks with you, not just because of the view, but because of the mix of effort, reward, thrill, and awe. A place that no travel guide could ever truly describe the way it actually feels to sit up there.

A few days later, I decided to spend a day entirely on my own. Nati needed a little break from all the tours, snorkelling and early mornings, and I had absolutely no problem with that.

On the contrary, I love my own company. While she spent the day relaxing at the Cairns Esplanade with our German friend, I set off. All by myself.

I booked my first whale-watching tour. And I was buzzing. Really buzzing. I could hardly sleep the night before. Whales had been at the top of my list since childhood – these giant, calm, majestic animals had always fascinated me. I booked a tour to Fitzroy Island, a small tropical island about 45 minutes by ferry from Cairns.

Early in the morning, it was still cool, I had my hood up and wore a light jacket – I boarded the boat. While almost everyone else stayed inside, warming up and peering out fogged-up windows, I sat outside on the deck. Sure, it was freezing. But hey – I'd paid for this tour, and I wanted to see everything. I'm not the type to hide inside when there's adventure waiting out there. Life's never boring with me, at least not when there are whales possibly in sight.

The sea sparkled in the morning light, a few seagulls followed the boat, and even though I was freezing, I was full of anticipation. Then it happened. A shout from the other end of the boat:

*»There! Whales!«*

I jumped up, ran to the railing, and there they were. Humpback whales. Just metres from the boat. Their backs shimmered in the sun, they surfaced, rolled, and then a giant flipper slapped the water several times, loudly. It looked like they were waving at us. I couldn't believe what I was seeing. My heart was racing. Tears welled up in my eyes. Actual tears of joy. I had dreamed of this moment for so long. Later I read that whales often do this so-called "tail slapping" to communicate, or maybe just for fun. To me, it was the warmest welcome I'd ever received.

Soon after, we reached Fitzroy Island. The tour guides gave us a few hours to explore the island on our own before the ferry returned in the afternoon.

Fitzroy Island is small, quiet, lush, and stunning. No big attractions, no souvenir shops, no entertainment. Just dense tropical vegetation, white coral beaches, and crystal-clear water. I walked barefoot along the shore, let the sun warm my face, and could spot turtles gliding through the water right from the beach. The water was so clear you could even see colourful fish without getting wet. At some point, I grabbed a cold Coke from the island's small restaurant, sat down in the shade and just… breathed. I think I had rarely been so present in the moment as I was that day.

In the late afternoon, the boat took us back to Cairns. Nati and our friend picked me up at the harbour, and my salty ocean adventure wasn't quite over yet. Back at the hostel, Nati had to spend nearly three hours untangling my hair. I have very fine, delicate strands – the kind you might call fairy hair, but about ten times as much as a normal person. A combination that doesn't exactly play well with salt, wind, and waves. The result? A matted, bird's-nest disaster. A tragic tale of haircare failure. Luckily, I've learned a few tricks by now: leave-in conditioner, a wide-tooth comb, patience, and a good friend with strong arms.

If you ever make it to Cairns, take your time. Not just for the Reef or the city itself, but for everything quietly surrounding it. For the small, green wonders you won't find on postcards. Make your way to Cape Tribulation, where the oldest rainforest in the world meets the ocean, and it feels like nothing has changed there in thousands of years. Ride the old, creaky train line up through the mountains to Kuranda and watch the scenery roll by as if you've slipped into another century. Or stand out in the middle of nowhere at night and just look up—because in this corner of Australia, you'll see stars you'll never catch a glimpse of in Europe.

Slowly, things were getting serious. At the start of our trip, Nati and I had saved a little over 10,000 euros between us, and that money had carried us this far: tours, hostels, our car, petrol, food, the occasional bottle of wine, and plenty of adventure. But we knew it wouldn't last forever. We needed a farm job. Even though we didn't know what the future would hold after this year, I wanted to be prepared. Nati was fairly certain that she'd return to Germany after around eleven months. For her, Australia was a big adventure, just one exciting chapter. But for me, I felt more and more that a whole new book might be opening here. One I wasn't ready to close.

So I wanted to play it safe. To get a second Working Holiday visa, we needed to do three months of farm work—officially documented, out in the middle of nowhere, somewhere within Australia's regional zones. No office, no casual job in a café, just heat, mud, early mornings, and hard work.

We were now at the point where it was time to leave Cairns. But before we turned our backs on the tropical north for good, there was one last highlight on our list, something that had been marked on our map for a long time: the Daintree Rainforest.

A place that doesn't just look like a jungle – it is a jungle. One of the oldest in the world, even older than the Amazon.

The Daintree is green in every imaginable shade, humid, alive, and in many places so dense that you can barely see the sky. The air was thick and warm, every step crackled over damp leaves, and at times it felt like you weren't the one doing the observing , but the one being watched.

Our goal was clear: crocodiles. Or, if we were really lucky – a cassowary. This bird looks like it came straight out of prehistoric times: almost human-sized, with strong legs, black shaggy feathers, and a striking blue-coloured neck. On its head, it wears a kind of horn-like crest, like a dinosaur helmet from another era. The cassowary is considered one of the most dangerous birds in the world because its dagger-like claws can cause serious harm if it feels threatened.

But that day, there was none of that. It appeared in front of us out of nowhere, crossed the path in long strides as if the rainforest belonged to it – which, to be fair, it probably does, and disappeared into the thick undergrowth again. No growling, no puffing up, no threatening gestures. Just a quick glance, then it was gone. And us? We just stood there, half fascinated, and half in disbelief – once again reminded that Australia is no petting zoo.

We drove our car through the water, feeling very heroic, kept our eyes peeled for crocodiles, got soaked walking through the rainforest, and stood on the beach in pouring rain.

Honestly? There's hardly anything more beautiful than tropical rain. The kind of rain that doesn't give you a warning, it just crashes down on you. One minute the sun is shining, and the next, a thunderclap, as if someone tipped a bucket over the sky. Big, heavy drops hammer the warm ground, and barefoot you can feel the asphalt steaming while little streams of water run down the sides of the road. It's one of those moments when you probably should look for shelter, but you just don't want to.

Because it feels good. Warm. Freeing. You stop walking, laugh, tilt your face to the sky and let the rain run over your skin. No shivers, no cold. Just that short, dense downpour that wraps everything like a misty curtain, and disappears as quickly as it came. What's left behind is the earthy scent of leaves, soil, and summer.

On the way back, we stopped in Palm Cove – a small but irresistible place, lined with tall, lush green palm trees and a beach that looked like something straight out of a movie scene. The soft sand formed gentle dunes, and the sea rolled in with a steady rhythm, each wave lapping at the shore as if inviting us to simply savour the moment.

By chance, we ran into two Germans – a warm, charming couple we instantly clicked with. We spent the afternoon together dipping into the cool waves, even though warning signs about crocodiles were clearly posted along the shore. Still, the heat and the promise of a refreshing swim proved too tempting to resist.

We laughed, swam, and splashed through the water like nothing in the world could stop us. To top off the day, I tried fresh passionfruit for the very first time, sold at a little roadside stall, and I was instantly hooked. That fruity sweetness, combined with the coolness of the water still clinging to my skin, made the whole experience utterly irresistible. We wrapped up the afternoon sitting on the beach, chatting as the last rays of sunlight slowly faded into evening, and we all felt that life here moved at a different, more relaxed pace.

Afterwards, we made our way back to Cairns – another long drive, following public roads, always accompanied by the constant sound of the ocean and the sense that each passing kilometre was gently wrapping up the day. For me, it had been one of those days that offered the perfect mix of nature, spontaneous company, and unexpected little joys – the kind of day that felt exactly how life should.

The next morning, the time had come. The moment we truly closed the Cairns chapter. We packed our things, completely emptied out and repacked Goldi, filled up the tank, and hit the road. Southbound.

The East Coast lay ahead of us: Gold Coast, Brisbane, Surfers Paradise, Sunshine Coast, Fraser Island, Byron Bay… names that until then had only existed on maps or in our minds, and that we were now about to fill with our own memories. I still remember looking out the window as we drove off and thinking,

*»Haven't we just arrived?«*

It didn't feel like weeks had passed, more like days. Our time in Cairns had flown by. Maybe because we had truly lived every moment of it. Everything now lay behind us – the steamy hiking tracks through tropical rainforest, our first time snorkelling at the Great Barrier Reef, whale watching, night markets, breakfasts in a camping chair with palm trees in view, hot showers after freezing waterfalls, car conversations, laughter, wonder, exhaustion, and euphoria.

We had truly made the most of this chapter and were ready for the next. We didn't yet know what lay ahead, which places would surprise us, which people we'd meet, or what challenges we'd face. But that was the beauty of it.

We left Cairns with both a smile and a heavy heart, grateful for everything we'd experienced, and excited for everything still to come.

# CHAPTER EIGHT

FROM NORTH TO SOUTH

The road stretched out ahead of us, the ocean to our left, and the thought of all the places still waiting for us made everything feel light. We didn't have a fixed destination, just the East Coast. Just this vast stretch of Australia with so many names attached to it: Airlie Beach, Fraser Island, Noosa, Gold Coast, Byron Bay. But none of that really mattered. What counted was: we were on the move. Finally back on the road, and this time with no plan at all.

After the intense time in the tropical north, the freedom of travelling again felt like a fresh start. No big expectations, no "We absolutely have to see…" Just drive, stop when it feels right, move on when your gut tells you it's time.

Mission Beach was one of those places that suddenly shows you what life can feel like, when you're truly living it. Not like a holiday, not like a break from reality, but like a whole new chapter. It was one of those places that immediately slowed us down. We had no real plan, no set goal, and that was exactly what made it so perfect.

Our days started slowly, usually around half past seven, not woken by an alarm but by the sun pushing its way through the car window, or the heat that builds up inside once the first rays warm the paintwork. Opening the windows only helped for so long – getting up was the only real option.

Our morning routine was simple: fresh water from the canister on the roof, brushing our teeth with a view of palm trees, sunscreen on our faces, hair brushed – done. No make-up, no mirror, no rush.

Back in Germany, I never would've imagined that. You'd rarely leave the house without make-up. But here, it was different – no one cared what you looked like, not the locals, not the other travellers. Aussies just lived. Naturally, effortlessly, and it was contagious.

∫

During the day we explored beaches, walked through national parks, swam in rivers, stopped wherever it felt right. Especially in places like Mission Beach, where white sandy shores meet deep green rainforest, you quickly lose all sense of time.

One day, we watched riders galloping along the water's edge with their horses, a scene straight out of a film. Despite all the lightness of the moment, a sense of caution always lingered.

In northern tropical Australia, especially between October and May, you have to think twice about where you go for a swim. That's where they live: box jellyfish.

Tiny, almost invisible, barely larger than a fingernail, but deadly. Their tentacles contain a venom so potent that a single touch can be enough to overwhelm the cardiovascular system in no time. The pain is excruciating, like fire burning beneath your skin. Often, there's only a small window of time to get to a hospital, sometimes just minutes. These inconspicuous jellyfish are among the most dangerous marine creatures in the world. Many beaches have warning signs, some even have protective nets, but the uneasy feeling remains when stepping into the water. Especially around regions like Cairns, Mission Beach, or the coastal areas near Townsville. Still, that didn't stop us from moving on.

A few days later, another little adventure awaited us: we caught the ferry from Townsville to Magnetic Island, hoping to finally see koalas in the wild. Not in a zoo, not as part of a guided tour – but on our own, out in the real Aussie bush.

The crossing took just twenty minutes. We had booked our tickets online in advance – better safe than sorry, especially since the ferry tends to get quite busy during peak season. Once there, everything was straightforward. No guided tour, no schedule. We wanted to decide for ourselves where to go, what to see, how long to stay. Just explore the island on our own – beaches, bays, walking tracks, nature.

Our goal: the "Forts Walk," one of the island's most popular trails, not only because of its historic World War II ruins, but also because it's said to be one of the best spots to see koalas. Or so we thought.

Reality: the sun was relentless, the track hilly, dusty, at times quite steep, and not a koala in sight. We stopped again and again, scanning the trees, searching for that familiar silhouette. But there was nothing. Just eucalyptus and heat. Our water bottles were running low, and so was our motivation. We were tired, sticky, sweaty.

On the verge of giving up. Until Nati suddenly stopped. Not a word. Just a quiet finger pointing upwards, and there she was: a koala mum, curled up on a branch, completely relaxed. The best part? A tiny head peeking out from behind her back. A baby. It looked at us curiously, then shyly hid behind its mother again. We just stood there. For minutes. Silent. Breathing softly. Everything around us was still, except for our thoughts, which started dancing. We had really found one – our koala. In the wild. And in that exact moment, the two of us turned into two completely ecstatic lunatics. Out of pure joy. We jumped around, half-dancing on the spot, whisper-shouting,

»*Oh my god, look at that!*«, and
»*He's so cute!*«

Nati and I just couldn't calm down. We were in hysterics, whispering to each other at least ten times how unbelievably adorable he was, while the two koalas up in the tree probably thought:

»*What the hell is wrong with those two?*«

At the end of the day, completely exhausted but happy, we found a small bench by the side of the path somewhere in the middle of the bush. The sun was low in the sky, dusk was setting in, but it was far from quiet.

On the contrary, Australia's birdlife was only just getting started. It sounded as if a hundred different species were all chattering at once, loudly discussing the day. And right in the middle of it all: the kookaburras. These birds are true Aussie originals. Not just because of how they look, but because of their "laughter". Their call actually sounds like a shrill, almost hysterical laugh that echoes through the entire forest. Hard to believe, but absolutely true. Once you've heard it, you'll never forget it. We just sat there, listening to this wild concert, barely able to take in how alive this place felt. Like a jungle – only on a tiny island off the coast of Australia.

An hour later, our ferry took us back to Townsville. Tired but content, we leaned against the railing and let the day gently come to an end. The sea was calm, the boat glided quietly across the dark blue water, and then it appeared: the sunset. The clouds on the horizon turned a deep, rich orange – like ripe persimmon, almost coppery, streaked with reddish veins like a sliced-open pomegranate. It felt as though someone had dimmed the light and turned up the colours instead. The sea reflected the fiery orange, the silhouettes of the surrounding hills sank into warm light. A view so breathtaking, it felt unreal, even though we were right there in the middle of it.

When we arrived in Townsville, we happened to find a public shower, and not just any shower, but one with actual hot water.

Anyone who's been travelling through Australia for a while knows: that's almost like winning the lottery. Most beachside showers are freezing cold or don't work at all, but this one was warm, clean, free, and came at exactly the right time. We were completely sweaty from hiking, from the heat, and from the salty film on our skin. And suddenly, there we were, standing under hot water in the middle of a small city in tropical northern Australia, and for a moment, it felt like being at a spa.

After showering, we found a public barbecue spot and cooked ourselves something to eat – probably our usual fried potatoes with capsicum and that famous cheese-and-chive dip from Woolworths.

A few days later, we continued heading south. Our next destination: Airlie Beach. The drive there dragged on a bit, but eventually we arrived and rolled into the small, lively town. Airlie Beach is incredibly popular among backpackers – no surprise, since it sits right at the gateway to one of the most stunning places in the world: the Whitsunday Islands. The town itself isn't big, but it has a special charm. Palm trees, colourful cafés, heaps of young people with backpacks, thongs, and sunglasses. You can feel the anticipation in the air, almost everyone arriving here is planning a trip to the Whitsundays. We wanted to go too, though we hadn't booked anything yet. First, we just wanted to settle in.

What we quickly realised, however, was that finding a free campsite in or around Airlie Beach is pretty much impossible. The area is tightly regulated, and wild camping is technically not allowed. In Australia, illegal camping can cost you up to 660 AUD in fines. So, we tried to be as discreet as possible. We parked in a posh residential area on a hill, awkwardly slanted, half hidden, half panicked. Quickly boiled some potatoes on the gas cooker, half raw of course, while a dog barked at us non-stop through the fence for nearly half an hour. Not exactly subtle. We tried to eat quietly, breathe quietly – though we were probably the exact opposite of discreet. That night was a full-on balancing act. Because of the slope, Nati kept rolling onto me in her sleep, squashing the air out of my lungs while I lay half-crushed under pillows and blankets. But hey – we were warm, we were there, and we had something to look forward to.

The next morning, at exactly six o'clock, our booked tour to the Whitsundays began, and to be honest, it exceeded everything. Still half-asleep, we stood at the harbour with takeaway coffees and sunscreen in hand, as the sky slowly shifted from deep blue to soft pink. The air was warm, salty, and full of expectations.

As the boat finally pulled away, the first rays of sunlight spilled across the glittering sea, which lay still as if it were welcoming us. Whitehaven Beach was our destination – a place everyone raves about, yet none can truly describe until they've been there.

The moment we arrived felt like something out of another life. The sand was so white it almost hurt to look at. Powdery, soft, finer than any flour. With every step, our feet sank in as though we were walking through warm icing sugar. And the water? A mix of turquoise, azure, and a blue that usually only exists in Photoshop. So clear, you could see the seabed even in knee-deep water. We wandered barefoot through paradise, taking – as always, a thousand photos. But somehow, this time, it was more than just that. It was one of those days when everything felt right, inside and out.

Later, we went snorkelling around the nearby islands. We were surprised, not just by the underwater world itself, but by how quiet everything became the moment we slipped into the sea. Our movements slowed, the noise of the day disappeared. Suddenly, there was only the sound of breathing through a snorkel, and wonder. Millions of fish in every colour. Schools moving as one, in perfect synchrony. Between the corals, tiny flashes of light – anemones, starfish, maybe even a clownfish. We floated, weightless and awestruck, lost between light reflections, colours, and the constant thought: We're really here.

Back on the boat for lunch, there were cold drinks, fresh fish, and a spot on the deck with views across the open sea. We sat barefoot on wooden benches, salt still on our skin, sun on our faces. Nobody said much, but no words were needed. Everything just felt right. Calm. Effortless. For a few hours, it was all simply… perfect. Australia, you leave us speechless.

When we returned from the Whitsundays that afternoon, it felt like we were carrying a little piece of a dream with us. Back in Airlie Beach, we drove a bit further until we found a small, secluded campsite. There, under palm trees, with the last sunlight on our skin and the sound of the coast in the background, we let the day come to an end – exhausted, happy, and with the feeling of being at the right place at the right time.

The next day, we decided to make up for a place we had missed on the way down: Bowen Beach. Just north of the

Whitsundays and definitely worth a detour. We spent the entire day at the beach, sifting through the shallow water for shells, crawling between rocks, jumping over stones and simply enjoying this quiet, laid-back day. Bowen was different. Slower, quieter, and that's exactly what we needed.

In the evening, we received the most beautiful gift of all: the most spectacular sunset we had ever seen – yes, I know, I've probably said that five times already, but this one really was the champion of all sunsets! The sky was full of clouds shaped like small waves, and the colours – deep pink, vibrant orange, warm reds, cast a surreal light over everything around us. It's hard to put into words. Maybe it truly was the most beautiful sunset of my life, even though Australia throws moments like this at you almost daily. Nearly every evening, and each time we just stood there, speechless.

We stayed overnight in Bowen and set off early the next morning towards Cape Hillsborough – a small hidden gem on the East Coast, surprisingly overlooked by many.

The area is a protected national park with dense rainforest, rocky bays, and a long, unspoilt beach where kangaroos hop by at sunrise. Yes, real kangaroos, leaping across the sand with their huge bounds. The scene feels almost staged, but it's completely real, and perhaps that's what makes it so magical.

There's only a small accommodation in the area, barely any mobile reception, and hardly any tourists. That's exactly what makes Cape Hillsborough one of those rare places that feels like a well-kept secret, a "must-see" before everyone else finds out about it.

It's especially known, at least among those in the know, for a moment many associate more with the famous Lucky Bay on the south coast of Western Australia. There too, you can watch kangaroos at the beach in the early morning or late evening – on blindingly white sand that almost looks like freshly fallen snow. But Cape Hillsborough is no less impressive. Here too, the kangaroos casually hop across the beach early in the morning, while the sky is slowly bathed in soft light. And then there's this one rock rising out of the water, right in view when you look straight out to sea, and I couldn't help but immediately think of the film 'The Shallows' – one of my favourite movies. The rock looks like a "pregnant woman" floating on her back in the water. Maybe I'm being silly. Or maybe I just have too much imagination.

We then took countless photos of the adorable kangaroos on the beach, walked barefoot along the entire bay and simply let our minds wander. It was another one of those rare moments when you're not thinking, not planning, not analysing, just being. The nature, the light, the sounds, the soft sand under our feet, it all seemed to be in perfect harmony. As on so many days during this trip, we realised how little it actually takes to be truly happy. You don't need much – you just need to be present. Right there, in the moment. That's what Australia gives you almost every single day: the chance to block everything else out and feel life the way it's meant to be – real, simple and free.

After our time in Cape Hillsborough, we continued along the coast, with new adventures in our backpacks and the desire to miss nothing. We stopped at every place that called out to us: Yeppoon, Emu Park, Rockhampton, hidden national parks, Gladstone, Agnes Water, Bundaberg, Hervey Bay, and of course Rainbow Beach with its famous rainbow-coloured stairs. A proper selfie hotspot, clearly showing: the tourists have arrived – and we were right in the middle of it. After around two weeks full of exploring, road trip vibes and stops at beaches, cafés and lookouts, we finally reached the place I had been looking forward to the most: Noosa National Park.

*»Finally the Sunshine Coast!«*

And all I wanted was to surf. I'd been watching the surfers for days, and now I wanted to get into the water myself. Just watching? That wasn't an option anymore. Nati was instantly on board, so it was clear: we needed a surfboard. No hesitation, no debate – the decision was made.

So we scrolled through Facebook Marketplace, Gumtree and similar sites once again. And sure enough, that very same day I came across a board that didn't just look great, but gave off exactly the vibe I'd been searching for. Simple, in a rich shade of blue, with a white stripe down the middle and a small whale design near the fins – understated, but somehow special.

I could hardly believe it: my very own surfboard. How cool is that? Back in Germany, this would never have even been a thing. Surfing just doesn't play a major role there. Probably because we live in a country where it feels like winter for ten out of twelve months. Instead of catching waves, people are more into football, indoor sports or winter activities like skiing or ice skating. It's a different world – not worse, just entirely different.

But here in Australia, surfing wasn't just something people did, it was part of everyday life. Even in the smallest coastal towns, you'd see surf shops, rental vans and people strolling around barefoot with boards under their arms – tanned, relaxed, casual. It wasn't a trend, it was a lifestyle, deeply rooted in the culture and almost second nature.

We decided that one board would be enough for now. If we ever wanted to surf at the same time, we could just rent a second one, there were rental stands on pretty much every corner.

The rest of the day was all about sun, saltwater and waves. We spent hours in the ocean, fighting the current, practising our pop-ups, falling, laughing, trying again, and savouring every single moment. It wasn't about being good at it – it was about being there. Being part of that rhythm, and the calm within the chaos.

By the evening, we were wrecked, but in the best possible way. Our skin tight from the sun, hair full of salt, bodies blissfully tired. No small talk needed. We just crashed into bed, content and worn out. I knew this had been more than just another day at the beach. It was another step into a life that finally felt like mine.

Over the next few days, we explored Noosa and the Sunshine Coast. There was so much to discover: stunning walking trails winding along the coastline, lookout points like Hell's Gate, charming cafés serving fresh smoothie bowls, and little boutiques where you could browse for hours. One of our favourite moments: we were walking along a little trail right next to Noosa Beach when we suddenly spotted something high up in the trees. *»A koala!«* Curled up on a branch, fast asleep in the afternoon sun. Just like that.

After our surprise koala encounter in Noosa, we enjoyed another gorgeous sunset on the beach and let the evening drift to a peaceful close.

Early the next morning, we hit the road again and headed towards Brisbane. On the way, we made a stop at the Glass House Mountains. The scenery was simply breathtaking: endless green farmland, gentle hills, grazing horses and cows, and in the background, the iconic mountains. It felt like an idyllic blend of my rural homeland and the tropical beauty of Australia. This connection to nature and the countryside reminded me of my own childhood and only deepened my love for this country.

I'd always been a water child. The ocean held a special kind of pull for me, long before I was even aware of what it meant. My mum later told me that even during my birth, everything took a little longer. The doctors joked that I was just too comfortable in the amniotic fluid, as if I didn't want to come out at all. It took eight, maybe nine hours until I finally entered the world. Maybe it was just a coincidence, or maybe it was the first sign of how calming the element of water has always been for me. To some, it might sound strange, but to me, there's hardly a more peaceful moment than being underwater. Whether I'm snorkelling or diving, as soon as the sounds of the outside world disappear and all

I can hear is the steady rhythm of my own breath through the mouthpiece, I feel completely calm. It's as if my brain hits reset. No thoughts, no overstimulation, no distractions, just silence, vastness, and a deep sense of contentment.

No wonder I fell in love with this country. Australia felt like a long-lost puzzle piece that had finally found its place. The coast, the nature, the laid-back way of life, it all just fit.

After leaving the Glass House Mountains behind, we continued our journey towards Brisbane, with the feeling that this road trip wasn't just taking us across the map, but deeper into a life that was starting to feel more and more like home. But before we could fully dive into the city life, the reality of road tripping caught up with us.

Nati and I desperately needed a shower. The sun, the saltwater, the sand — all of it was still clinging to us, and we were beginning to feel more like dusty vagabonds than actual people. So we tried to book a hostel at the last minute, with no luck. Brisbane was packed with backpackers, and every place was fully booked. So we stopped in a quiet residential area just outside the city. And then it happened: the most glamorous non-shower of our lives. Nati and I quickly threw on our bikinis, a little bit of decency, at least — and set our almost empty water canister on the kerb. There we stood, in the middle of a suburban street in Australia, crouched under a dripping tap, scrubbing the salt from our hair and washing the road trip off our skin with the last bit of energy we had left.

Afterwards, we drove another 45 minutes to a free campsite nearby, where we spent the night. Only the next morning did we head back into the city.

Brisbane was vibrant, friendly, sunny. We strolled through the streets, took in the view from the lit-up Story Bridge, and explored cafés, parks, and little shops. It was one of the most beautiful cities we'd seen in Australia. Thankfully, we managed to score a hostel room for two nights and used the time to rest and recharge.

Then came the call we'd been waiting for: a farmer from the Atherton Tablelands finally offered us a job. We didn't hesitate for a second, even though the drive would take almost 20 hours and cover more than 1,600 kilometres.

We knew this was our chance, to extend our visa and give our travel budget a break. He said we could start working straight away, but only under one condition:

*»You have to be here in two days and start working!«*

No further details, no wiggle room. We mentioned that we were currently in Brisbane – nearly 1,700 kilometres away. But he didn't seem to care. He just needed workers. We had to go. No time for consideration or understanding, just efficiency. We knew this wouldn't be an easy decision. But honestly, we didn't have a choice. Our bank account looked miserable, we'd been counting every dollar for days, already calculating every expense: fuel, food, accommodation. A job was long overdue. And not just that, we also had our second year visa in the back of our minds. We knew we had to act now if we wanted a real chance at another year in Australia. So we packed our things—exhausted, but with a clear goal in sight.

The tiredness still clung to our bones, but it didn't matter anymore. What mattered was getting there. We had no idea what to expect. The way the farmer spoke on the phone already hinted at something, not exactly friendly, but we didn't have the capacity to question it. This was about survival. It wasn't the job we had dreamed of. But it was the one we needed.

Sometimes, you don't make decisions because they feel right, but because they're necessary. But even on the way there, a quiet feeling crept in, that this part of our journey wouldn't be defined by ease and freedom, but by hard work, little sleep, and the challenge of dealing with people who don't always play fair.

# CHAPTER NINE

ARRIVING IN THE UNKNOWN

We were back on the road. This time from Brisbane all the way back to Atherton, an endless drive that left us tired and drained. By the time we finally arrived at the farm, the farmer was already waiting for us. He briefly introduced himself, showed us the room we'd be living in for the next few weeks, and gave us a rough rundown of our tasks: from seven in the morning until five in the evening, day in, day out.

At the share house we were meant to call home, we met a few other backpackers – an English couple and a German girl named Melanie, who was travelling solo. Melanie was a real bundle of joy, and we clicked instantly. In our free time, we were always off doing something together and quickly became a tight-knit trio.

But the work on the farm was tough. We stood on a

harvester, a large machine, sorting potatoes in pouring rain. The farmer seemed to have it in for me: while everyone else could throw away the rejected potatoes, I had to climb down and pick up the good ones again, all in the middle of that downpour. The farmer was a terrible person, always late with payment and never sending the necessary payslips we needed for our second-year visa. It was frustrating, but an experience that made us stronger.

Still, we managed to find some bright moments. On our days off, we drove to Cairns with Melanie, enjoyed the scenery, and even landed a cash-in-hand job through her, painting the fence of an Airbnb house. The owner was incredibly friendly, brought us lunch, and paid us in cash – a real highlight in the midst of a tough time.

The weeks went by, and although the nearest supermarket was over an hour away, we made the most of every weekend grocery trip and the drives through the mountains. Despite all the setbacks, it somehow felt good in the end, because we stuck together, built new friendships, and managed to find something beautiful even in the middle of exhaustion.

Of course, after a long day of work, a shower was always a must. The farmer had set up an old, half-abandoned-looking house with a shower just behind the share house, specifically for the backpackers. One day, I walked in, not suspecting a thing, and in that moment, my heart nearly stopped. A massive python was casually draped across the shower rod, slithering along as if it owned the place. I screamed at the top of my lungs, flung the door open and bolted back to the share house. The others stood there stunned while I struggled to catch my breath, panicked and shaking. Nati just looked at me, raised an eyebrow and said dryly,

*»That was probably the fastest shower you've ever had in your life. Wow.«*

I was still in shock, somewhere between laughing and crying. We immediately called the farmer, begging him to get rid of the snake. He actually showed up, completely calm, as farmers tend to be, and simply said we should be glad it wasn't a brown snake.

*»This one's harmless.«* he added.
*»Won't do you any harm.«*

And then, as if it was the most normal thing in the world, he asked if we wanted to hold it. Melanie and I looked at each other. What did we have to lose? You only live once. So we stood there, with a metre-long python draped over our arms. Nati, meanwhile, had already backed away several metres, hands in the air, shouting,

*»Yeah, I am not touching that thing!«*

We all burst out laughing – and with that, the shower was officially reclaimed.

Just a few days later, a terrible smell began to spread across the property. It was truly awful. So Nati, Melanie and I went on a mission to figure out where it was coming from. The trail led us to a massive water tank, and when we lifted the lid, we saw it: a dead possum. Wedged between the lid and the tank, completely decomposed. We tried to get it out with a huge iron pole, and at one point it nearly fell right onto Melanie's head. We couldn't stop laughing. It was disgusting, gross, and exactly the kind of backpacker story you never forget.

∿

A few weeks later, when the potato season came to an end and the farmer barely had any work left for us anyway, we decided to quit. The three of us – Melanie, Nati and I, were in full agreement: enough was enough. We had spent nine weeks on the farm, but maybe only worked four or five of them. The rest of the time was filled with waiting, hoping, hanging around. Our first farm experience? Terrible. But life goes on. When one door closes, another one opens.

The moment we quit, it felt right. So Nati and I got the car ready for the road again. We went shopping, filled up the tank, packed everything carefully, and made a final decision: we were leaving Cairns and the surrounding area. It was our last day driving through the lush green mountains, through the deep, vibrant countryside of northern Australia.

A few hours later, we reached a small free campsite in Innisfail, right next to a massive banana plantation. It was our final meet-up with a good friend from Germany, someone we had known for many years. We'd reconnected in Australia and now, one last evening together before our paths would split for a long time.

We parked our two cars side by side, unfolded our camping chairs and finally took a deep breath. Our friend had a rooftop tent – pretty cool actually. In the morning, you just unzip it, get a breath of fresh air and look straight out into the world from your window. You can see everything. Who's already awake, whether the sun's up yet, or whether it's still worth closing your eyes again. A bit like a bird in its nest, only with a view of the stars.

Dinner was the usual – pasta with green pesto, some chopped-up tomatoes, all served in a cheap plastic bowl from Kmart. The cheapest of the cheap, but somehow just right. No frills, no unnecessary luxury. Simple, filling, and exactly what we needed after a long day. If other backpackers had seen us, they probably would've nodded, knowingly. Because that's exactly why you become a backpacker: because you don't need all that excess.

The three of us sat there, looking up at the sky, saying nothing. Australia has this kind of silence, not the awkward kind, but one that feels full. Like a breath into the open. And honestly? If I had to choose between a techno-flooded night out with strobe lights and some sweaty guy with a towel over his shoulder, or a spot in a camping chair somewhere among palm trees, gazing up at the southern stars? Well… let's just say I've never voluntarily gone for the first option.

You might be wondering why we didn't travel together with our friend from Germany? But the answer is simple: Nati and I really wanted to travel on our own. When you're with someone 24/7, everything has to click — and it did. For me and Nati, there could never have been a better travel buddy. We'd always been close friends, but Australia? Australia brought us even closer together every single day.

The next morning, we woke up early, said goodbye to our friend, and all we wanted was a proper shower. But the only thing this campsite had was a water tap sticking out of the pavement. So we stood right underneath it, in our bikinis, washing our hair and our whole bodies. Right there on the car park. It's probably the kind of thing you only do once in your life. Or so we thought!

Then a woman walked by, saw us, grinned, and asked,
*»Can I take a photo?«* I just replied dryly,
*»sure, I don't care«*.

Because I honestly didn't. As long as we were clean and didn't "stink" anymore, I was happy.

It's in moments like that when you realise how much you start to appreciate the little things: a daily shower, hot or cold. A roof over your head. Something to eat. A fridge. Things you never really question back home. But on the road? They suddenly feel like pure gold.

We jumped into the car, shut the doors, and hit the road again, heading south, back the way we'd come weeks earlier. Back toward Brisbane. That's where we'd paused our journey, before the potato farm had taken us up north. We didn't know exactly what was waiting for us, but one thing was certain: we desperately needed money. Our travel funds were almost empty, but the adventure was far from over. We didn't want to spend weeks getting back to Brisbane again. We wanted to pick up right where we'd left off.

Of course, we still needed a new farm job and wanted to save money, so we drove across inland Queensland, stopping at every second farm, getting out and asking directly:

*»Hi, are you looking for workers right now?«*

That was our go-to line. Most of the time, the farmers shook their heads politely. But we didn't give up.

After about a week, we finally found a farm that at least offered us accommodation in exchange for our help. It wasn't a proper paid job, but we could stay for free, together with other backpackers. Five hours of work a day in return for a roof over our heads, a kitchen, and new connections.

The farm belonged to an older couple who ran a small plantation. We harvested custard apples, pruned trees and helped plant young mango trees. The work wasn't hard, everything was relaxed, and the couple was incredibly warm-hearted. On Saturdays, the older man even drove us to the supermarket in his big bus so we didn't all have to go separately, and he casually handed us a hundred dollars each time. A lovely gesture we never expected, but we truly needed it.

The other backpackers were almost all French, plus a German couple, it was a wonderfully colourful bunch. In the evenings, we all sat together, cooked, drank wine, and played cards. It was one of those unexpectedly beautiful chapters that shows you: sometimes a bit of community is all it takes to feel at home.

But after three weeks, we both knew it was time to move on. Not just pause, but move forward. Earn money, finish our 88 farm days for the second visa, and then take new paths. Keep travelling, keep dreaming, keep exploring Australia. While everything around us kept changing, places, people, thoughts – life back home in Germany seemed to continue at its usual pace.

Family and friends stayed in touch regularly. Nati spoke to

Eric almost every day, he missed her terribly. And she missed him. And then, almost in passing, we realised: five months had already gone by since we'd left Germany. Five months filled with adventure, detours, new perspectives, and everyday little wonders. In our minds, it felt like years. Hard to believe that it had all started with a single flight. Now we were right in the middle of it – not just in Australia, but in a life that felt so much more real than anything we'd known before.

Time flew by in the blink of an eye, but it left marks that would stay. And the next chapter was already waiting, ready to be discovered.

# CHAPTER TEN
## SUNSHINE & SKYSCRAPER

After three weeks, we said goodbye to the small family farm, feeling grateful for this peaceful, beautiful in-between chapter. We were ready to move on, back towards the Sunshine Coast.

Our first stop was the Eumundi Market, a true highlight in the region. The market takes place every Wednesday and Saturday and is packed with handmade products, art, jewellery, clothing, street food, and live music. It was a vibrant mix of creativity and Aussie spirit, and we spent hours strolling through the stalls, trying exotic food, chatting with locals, and picking up a few small souvenirs to take with us on our journey.

Then we continued on – to a place that had long been on our list: Surfers Paradise on the famous Gold Coast. Even the name sounded like freedom, sunshine, and waves – and that's exactly what we got, only better.

The Gold Coast greeted us with a kilometre-long golden beach, turquoise-blue water, and waves towering high above the shore. Skyscrapers towered behind the beach, creating an unforgettable scene: ocean and metropolis, side by side. Surfers Paradise was exactly what it sounded like, a paradise for surfers, sunseekers, night owls, and adventure lovers. There were countless surf shops, cafés, rooftop bars, beach promenades, and little boutiques.

A culinary highlight for us: the best Eggs Benedict in all of Australia! Nati and I agreed, this breakfast was hands down our absolute favourite. We usually ordered it with fresh salmon. For those unfamiliar: Eggs Benedict traditionally consists of two poached eggs on toasted bread or English muffins, topped with Hollandaise sauce, and typically served with ham, or in our case, delicious salmon. A creamy, savoury start to the day and just perfect after a night of surfing or a long morning walk on the beach.

Life here was vibrant, a little crazy, and totally contagious. We walked barefoot through the warm sand, watched the surfers catch wave after wave, and just felt free. It was loud, colourful, a bit over the top, but that was exactly what gave the place its charm.

For a few days, we simply went with the flow. Enjoyed the sunshine. The music, the people, the food, and the unique energy of the Gold Coast. As Nati and I slowly realised that life on the Gold Coast, while stunning, was far too expensive for our backpacker budget, we once again drove around aimlessly — out of the centre, back in, back out again, until we finally found a campsite where we could actually stay for five nights for free. Jackpot!

We were desperately searching for a job. It was frustrating. We were determined to complete our 88 days, and we needed to save money. Eric had already announced he'd be visiting soon, and by now it was already November. Time was flying—so fast, we could hardly keep up.

In the small town where we were camping at the time, we met another German girl in a supermarket car park. She was just as hopelessly looking for work as we were. Sabrina.

She was a free spirit too, believed in her dreams and worked hard to make them come true. What started as a random encounter quickly turned into a real friendship. We met her again later on, spent time together, and she remained one of our closest companions in Australia.

Of course, the free campsite had no showers. Not even a makeshift one tucked away behind a tree. But necessity is the mother of invention. And our saviour? A sprinkler. Right next to our spot was a little playground with a patch of grass, and there, every day, an automatic sprinkler came on—you know, the ones that gracefully sway from left to right, like they're straight out of an old American suburban movie.

And there we were: two backpackers in bikinis, in desperate need of a shower, and an even more desperate need to shave. So, at the crack of dawn, we crept onto the grass, hopping around the sprinkler like startled chickens, yelping every time the icy water hit us like a blast of icicles. It was bloody freezing. No joke. The water was so cold, it felt like every pore in my body immediately slammed shut. But we laughed so hard. I'll never forget that moment for the rest of my life. And then, mid-shave, I cut myself on the lower part of my leg. At first, I thought, no big deal. Two days later: it was inflamed. Hot, red, throbbing. Hello, first doctor's visit in Australia.

Of course, the night before, I googled what could happen if you leave a wound like that untreated. Spoiler: blood poisoning, amputation, death. I could already see myself lying in a hospital bed, with Nati crying beside me.

The next day, I managed to get an appointment straight away. Only problem: my English, when it came to medical terms, was about as useful as an umbrella in a hurricane. I stammered, gestured wildly, and probably painted half a picture with my hands. The doctor was patient, kind, and most likely used to patients who didn't speak perfect English. After examining me thoroughly, she explained slowly and in simple words what was wrong with me. I didn't understand every single detail, but enough to know: it wasn't anything serious. In the end, she casually added,

»Next time, you can also request a translator, by the way.«

Oh really? Thanks for the heads-up. Now that it was already over. Still, I was relieved. With a pack of antibiotics in hand, we left the clinic. I was supposed to take them for five days, then everything would be fine. No drama, no hospital, no big deal. Crisis averted.

That day, we ran a few errands. We went shopping, filled up the tank, and were just about to head back to find a quiet place to camp for the evening when suddenly a message popped up. Just like that, out of the blue. A job offer. For both of us. We stared at the screen. It almost sounded too good to be true. Paid work, a farm job, exactly what we had been looking for, in a region that counted towards our second-year visa. The message seemed legit, but also a little unexpected. Nati was sceptical. Understandably so. In Australia, you get plenty of offers, but not all of them are trustworthy. Sometimes they come with unfair conditions, dodgy accommodation, or just shady people.

But something about this one felt different. We couldn't quite put our finger on it, but the message stayed with us. What we didn't know at the time: this job, this place, this person who had messaged us, they would all end up shaping our Australian adventure in a way we never could have expected. It was the beginning of one of the most beautiful and defining chapters of our entire journey.

# CHAPTER ELEVEN
SOMEWHERE IN QUEENSLAND

Nati and I were standing in the middle of nowhere. One of those petrol stations out in the country where even the town sign looked like it had seen better days. The asphalt was cracked, the roof creaked quietly in the wind, and apart from us, there wasn't a single soul in sight. You couldn't be sure if the place was still in operation or just a backdrop for an old Aussie outback film. That's exactly when the message came through. A job offer.

Short, friendly, and straight to the point: asking if we were interested. We looked at each other. Interested? Of course. But we'd grown cautious. We'd received too many messages that promised the world and delivered nothing. Job offers where we were supposedly meant to start the next day, only to find out they were a mess – or flat-out fake. So, we replied straight away but kept it low-key. Yes, we were interested, but before agreeing to anything, we wanted all the details.

A few minutes later, the phone rang. A short phone call followed. The voice on the other end sounded calm, easy-going, somehow familiar. Mark – that's what he called himself. He ran a small family business nearby and was looking for a couple of helping hands. If we wanted, we could stop by the next day to have a look around. We ended the call, thanked him, and hung up. Then we sat there on the petrol station car park for a while, talking it through.

Later that evening, we drove to a small free campsite, deep in the bush, surrounded by eucalyptus trees and the chirping of crickets.

Over dinner, probably fried potatoes and capsicum from the pan again, we went through everything one more time. We were curious, but also tense. We knew how important this job was for us. Not just to earn some money, but because of the farm days. Without those 88 days, we wouldn't get our second visa.

*»We'll go check it out«,*

Nati finally said. If it's no good, we'll move on. But maybe… this time it's for real.

The next morning, we got up early, made a quick coffee, and hit the road. It was still cool outside, the air crisp. Somehow, it all felt open – like we were heading in a new direction without knowing where it might lead. By late morning, we turned onto a wide gravel road that led through open fields. Birds screeched as they flew over our car, a dog barked in the distance, and then we saw him. Mark.

He stood in front of a low building, casually leaning

against the open door of a small office, already waiting for us. In shorts, dusty boots, and with a big grin on his face. He reached out his hand like we were old mates. His handshake was firm, his voice warm.

*»Welcome guys«,* he said.

In that moment, we knew – this felt different. He took us straight across the property, pointing out the key spots: the little office, a massive shed, the vehicles, the tool racks, a few shipping containers. Everything looked tidy, but also kind of thrown together. Very Aussie. Practical, no-fuss, functional.

*»This is where you'll be tomorrow«,*

he said with a quick nod toward the shed as he kept walking ahead. We nodded, smiled, and quietly wondered what exactly "being here" was supposed to mean. Because even though he'd shown us around, one thing was still unclear: What exactly were we supposed to do? Was it fruit? Veggies? Machinery? Packing? Planting? Or something entirely different?

After a quick tour of the place, we sat down with him in his office. Mark talked a lot. He wanted to know where we were from, how long we'd been travelling, whether we'd done any farm work before. He laughed often, asked curious questions, and came across as genuinely interested – in that laid-back way that never felt intrusive. Eventually, maybe half an hour later, we carefully asked what exactly the job would involve. After all, we needed to know what we were getting ourselves into. He just grinned, leaned back in his chair, and said in the broadest Aussie accent:

*»Ah, don't worry. I'll explain everything later, at the Roadhouse. We're having dinner there tonight with my family. You'll meet everyone, and I'll tell you more about the job«.*

Alright then. Dinner at the Roadhouse with his family. Why not? Sounded unplanned, but kind of nice. We nodded, laughed, exchanged a glance, and probably both thought the same thing: Why not. We're in.

Mark was one of those blokes you only meet in Australia. A bit nuts, very direct, totally genuine, and because he didn't take life too seriously, we felt at ease right away.

So we drove to Cambooya – a tiny town you'd miss if you blinked. The moment I stepped into the pub, I thought: I'm in the right place. Loud, laughing, drunk Aussies in cowboy hats, beers in hand, darts sticking out of their backs, and western boots on their feet. Some were playing pool, others were glued to AFL, rugby, or soccer on massive TVs as if their lives depended on it. The food? Surprisingly good. Aussie pubs had never let us down. Their all-time favourite dish? Chicken Parmi. A crumbed chicken schnitzel topped with tomato sauce and melted cheese, served with chips and a cold beer. Hearty, rich, and just so bloody Aussie.

There we sat, in the middle of nowhere, surrounded by strangers who would soon become exactly what we never searched for but so deeply needed: a second family. Warm. Real. And our home for the next few weeks.

That night, Mark introduced us to his family: his son Dan, daughters Abby and Josie, and his wife Claire. From the first moment, they were welcoming, open, and honestly interested in us. It didn't feel like a job interview, it felt like being welcomed by friends. Mark's son, by the way, just putting it out there – was seriously good-looking. Really. But of course, he had a girlfriend. Typical. Didn't stop us from getting along brilliantly though.

Over dinner, Mark gave us a rough idea of what the job was about. He ran the "Machinery Agency" in Nobby, Queensland – a company that repairs, restores, spray-paints, and services agricultural feeding systems and machinery for farms. Whether it was welding, spare parts, or full rebuilds, the agency was the go-to place for farmers across Queensland whenever their machines needed fixing. It wasn't your typical farmwork. It was more like what you'd imagine as:

*»Behind the scenes of the Outbacks«.*

We spent the rest of the night at the pub, playing pool, laughing our heads off, and Mark? He paid for everything. No argument. We tried, we really did, but he just grinned and tapped his card at the counter like it was no big deal. Kind of like an Aussie sugar daddy, but with style. Nati and I were stunned. We barely had any money left. And then, just when we thought the night couldn't get any better, he handed us an envelope with our first week's pay. Over $800. In cash. Just like that.

*»Just a little motivation to get started tomorrow«* he said, with a wink. We were speechless. It was more than we'd made in weeks.

The next morning, we got straight to work. During that first week, we stayed on a nearby campground, nothing fancy, but it had showers, power, toilets. After a long day of physical labour, though, you want more than just functionality. You want somewhere to land. A home.

Mark had a solution for that, too. He knew a woman in town who had a spare room. Perfect timing, she said, she could rent it out for the exact months we'd be working for him. She was nice enough, no doubt. But it didn't take long to notice she had a very obvious drinking problem. She showed us the room, a small space in a plain house she shared with her dog, Sunny. And Sunny... was the sweetest little thing you could imagine. Big loving eyes, muddy paws, a soft coat, and a heart that was clearly starving for affection.

She never went for walks. Ever. Her owner simply couldn't be bothered. So we took over that job, happily. Nati and I fell in love with Sunny so quickly that we actually started thinking about taking her with us. Finding her a new home. A better one. Because the way she lived now? It was heartbreaking. She had to do her business in the tiny backyard because she rarely got out. When we were gone, she was stuck inside a cramped house with no space, no exercise, no life. Her owner was just lazy. Too indifferent to care.

In the evenings, she often came home drunk. Wobbly, slurring, holding a bottle of wine or a can of beer. More than once, she'd helped herself to our chocolate in the fridge. Sometimes she'd cook something for us, but there wasn't much else going on in her life anymore. It was sad. Empty, somehow. A bit pitiful.

One day, Nati even brought it up and told her that Sunny needed more walks and better care. But, as is often the case in these situations, all we got was a dismissive

"Yeah, yeah." Nothing changed. But something shifted in

us. Sunny waited for us every day. After work, we'd jump out of the car and Sunny? She'd zoom through the house like a little whirlwind, squealing, bouncing, spinning in circles the moment we picked up her lead. To her, we had become home.

That's how we spent our first six weeks in Cambooya – between welding shifts, early mornings and pure dog love. But now it's time to talk about the actual work.

Every morning, we'd drive about twenty minutes from our little town of Cambooya to Nobby – the place where Mark's workshop was. Or as he called it: the "Machinery Agency." We threw on our old, long-sleeve shirts from Kmart and stretched-out pants – not cute, but practical. Work started at 8 am and finished at 5 pm. Sounds like a normal routine. But, as so often in Australia, things went a little differently. Mark introduced us to his team – all locals, no backpackers.

*»We usually only take Germans« he said,*
*»at least you lot show up on time and actually work.«*

Thanks... I guess? The work itself wasn't hard. Nothing back-breaking. But we were there in the peak of summer – and in Nobby, that means up to 40 degrees. The sun was brutal. We tried to stick to the shade as much as possible, but sometimes we had to go outside – and out there, it felt like a bloody oven made of tin. Still, we often had a good laugh!

We sorted screws, cleaned greasy machine parts, spray-painted anything that didn't move, and slapped new labels onto massive feeding systems. Honestly, no one would believe how many stickers those machines needed – we're talking novel-length quantities!

Sometimes we even had to clean the machines from the inside. Which would've been fine... if it weren't for the spiders. Massive. Hairy. With glowing red eyes, or at least that's how it felt. One morning, I screamed, there was a spider right in front of me. Mark walked over laughing, rolled his eyes and crushed it with his finger. His finger! Excuse me?! Aussies really are built differently.

*»I mean, who even needs nerves?«*


We worked alongside four regular team members. There was Dan, Mark's son – good-looking, charming, unfortunately taken. Then Bailey, our secret favourite – super funny, easy-going, the kind of guy you'd instantly trust to break the rules with. And two older blokes, both kind and always willing to help. The whole crew felt like a small family. Every day, we'd all take "smoko" together, that Aussie-style coffee break with biscuits, banter and laughter.

Then there was Mr Carlsen. A ginger cat who strutted through the workshop like he ran the place. And, to be fair, he probably did. He was as much a part of the machinery agency as the toolboxes and the layers of dust on the shelves, and everyone loved him. Me too. At least until that one morning when I thought it'd be a good idea to pick him up. Maybe because he looked especially cute. Maybe because I hadn't had enough coffee yet to make rational decisions. Either way, I picked him up, and in that exact moment, Mr Carlsen decided to vomit up his freshly eaten breakfast. Right on my shirt. Warm. Mushy. Undeniably cat food. Cat vomit. First thing in the morning. In the middle of Queensland's stifling summer heat. The smell? A mix of old tuna and damp carpet. I smelt like a walking pet bowl all day. Nati couldn't stop laughing. Mark just said dryly,

*»Welcome to farm life.«*

And Mr Carlsen? He just strutted off like nothing had happened. But it's exactly those kinds of stories you end up telling again and again.

Between paint fumes, greasy hands and rusty tools, it wasn't the smooth workdays that stuck with us, it was the chaos, the characters, the unexpected. Besides the workshop jobs, Mark always had a million other things going on. No two days were ever the same. Sometimes we helped out in the office, sorting paperwork, checking orders, organising shelves, or giving his wife Claire a hand. Best part? The office had air con. I'm telling you, after hours of sweat and heat outside, that felt like a full-on spa treatment. Mark himself was a bit of everything: boss, mate, family man, walking whirlwind, and occasionally, a bit of a diva.

The moment he walked into the shed, suddenly everything became urgent. In the middle of whatever task you were doing, you'd hear him shout:

*»Where's the paint for the green machine?! Why isn't the welder in place?! I need someone to come with me. NOW!«*

Everyone internally rolled their eyes. No one said a word. But everyone was thinking the exact same thing.
We called it the Mark Effect, absolute chaos within seconds. But to be honest? That's exactly why we loved him. He genuinely looked after us. Whenever we'd been working

outside for hours in the blazing heat, he'd eventually show up and hand us an ice-cold Coke. No words, no fuss. Just like that. Exactly how you'd imagine a real "work dad".

---

Things got a bit emotional during the lead-up to Christmas. The holidays were approaching, and the thought of celebrating without our families and friends was hard to bear.

But Mark had two close friends – Hannah and Bob – and thanks to him, we got to know them too. Hannah and Bob liked us straight away, and they did something that still warms our hearts to this day: they invited us over for Christmas Eve dinner.

In Australia, Christmas is traditionally celebrated on the 25th of December. But they knew how much the 24th meant to us, how deeply we missed our families – so they organised a special Christmas dinner just for us.

Claire, possibly the kindest "Mum" in all of Australia, had of course pulled all the strings. She looked after us as if we were her own kids.

And there we were: on the 24th of December, sitting at a festively set table, surrounded by warm lights, laughter, and even a traditional German Christmas dinner, dessert and all.

I'm telling you, sometimes it's not the places that leave a mark on your heart. It's the people. People who truly see you. People who care. Even when, to them, you're just a backpacker who somehow landed in their world.

That evening, we were simply grateful. Because one thing is certain: holidays, birthdays, those special moments — they hit the hardest when you're travelling. When your loved ones aren't around. When you're far away, physically and emotionally. Most of the time, all you can do is grin and bear it. But sometimes... it's not so bitter, when there are good people nearby.

After celebrating our little "German" Christmas on the 24th, we got to experience a real Aussie Christmas the next day — with Mark, Claire, and the whole family. It was... different. Completely different. But that's exactly what made it so exciting and beautiful. Instead of candlelight and roast goose, there was sunshine, heat, laughter, and of course, lots of alcohol, which is basically mandatory at any Australian Christmas.

Mark and Claire had invited us to join them at the grandparents' place. What awaited us there was beyond anything we could have imagined. The house was tucked away on a vast farm property, surrounded by endless fields stretching all the way to the horizon. A wraparound veranda circled the entire building, an absolute dream of a home. On the back side of the house, overlooking the vast fields, hung an old brown wooden porch swing. Thick chains attached it to the roof of the veranda, and it swayed gently in the warm evening breeze. One of those classic swings you only ever see in old films. Not new, not modern, slightly worn, but full of charm. The wood creaked softly with every movement, and the gentle swinging matched the golden light slowly creeping across the fields as the sun began to set. It was one of those rare, perfectly peaceful moments where the world seems to hold its breath for just a second.

I remember sitting there, gently rocking back and forth, gazing into the evening light, and suddenly thinking of home. Of my mum. Of the garden I grew up in.

We had a swing too—not hanging like this one, but firmly planted on the ground, with the same soft, cosy cushions that practically called your name for an afternoon nap. I must have been 14 or 15, coming home tired from school, tossing my backpack in a corner somewhere, and heading straight out into the garden. Our swing sat among flowerbeds, bushes, and old trees. My mum's garden was like a little paradise—green, fragrant, and alive.

The grandparents welcomed us with open arms. Just the way you imagine grandparents to be: warm, kind, caring, with smiles that made you feel at home instantly. And as if all of that hadn't already been perfect, we even got to feed a newborn calf. So tiny, so clumsy, so incredibly adorable—we were absolutely smitten.

The food was a proper Aussie Christmas meal: grilled meats, crispy roast, seafood, fresh salads, pavlova with berries, and a traditional Christmas pudding for dessert. Everything was spread across long tables so everyone could help themselves—relaxed and informal, like a big family picnic. We sat together, laughing, chatting, enjoying the food and the laid-back atmosphere. It was simply lovely.

After lunch, it was time for presents. And yes, they had thought of us too. Two small, carefully wrapped gifts were waiting under the tree, just for Nati and me.

In that moment, it wasn't about the gift. It was about the gesture. The warmth. The feeling of belonging.

Mark was still our boss, technically speaking, but during those hours, it all felt like family. For a short while, we forgot how much it hurt not to be with our own families. The homesickness faded into the background. Because on that day, we'd found something else: a home away from home, and people who turned that day into a memory that would stay with us forever.

The rest of December flew by. Between work, laughter, family moments and the Australian sun, we barely noticed how quickly the days were passing.

Suddenly, New Year's Eve was just around the corner, and of course, in Australia, it was completely different from what we were used to. Sparklers? Poppers? Not a thing. In Australia, fireworks are banned due to the high risk of bushfires, especially in the scorching heat of summer. And it was hot. Even hotter than by the coast.

We thought about our New Year's traditions back home. Usually, we'd get together with our closest friends, everyone would bring food, we'd cook together, have a few drinks, play Monopoly, and just before midnight we'd wrap up warm and head out to the edge of the fields with our fireworks and poppers. Then, at the stroke of midnight: colourful explosions in the sky, laughter, hugs, and maybe a bit of drama. This time, everything was different. A true Aussie New Year's. Hot, wild, unforgettable.

Dan, Mark's son, had invited us to ring in the new year with him and his mates. In the middle of the bush. No club, no fireworks, no countdown on TV – just pick-up trucks, slabs of beer, and a river where everyone camped out. They were… let's just say: in top spirits. People were dancing barefoot on the trays of the trucks like there was no tomorrow – sweaty, wild, and completely unbothered by anything we'd known before. The music thumped through the speakers, beer cans flew through the air from hand to hand, and the dust twirled in the headlights like it was part of the party.

At first, Nati and I just stood there, watching the chaos unfold with a mix of slight disbelief and growing curiosity. But it didn't take long, a couple of drinks later and we were right in the thick of it. Laughing, dancing, singing at the top of our lungs.

One moment that will forever be burned into our memory was when Dan introduced us to one of his mates: Stuart. Short, slightly chubby, with short brown hair and a scruffy three-to-seven-day beard that looked like it had stayed by accident. His clothes were hanging off him at odd angles, like he'd pulled them straight from the laundry basket, and he had that particular vibe, like someone who hadn't looked in the mirror for days, but was fully convinced everything was on point. Classic bogan.

*»What's a bogan?«*

In Australia, it's a term used to describe people — usually from the country, with a very specific style: rough around the edges, loud, full of heart, not overly concerned with etiquette, and with a strong love for beer, flannelette shirts, old utes, and all kinds of dodgy antics. Think of it as the Aussie cousin of the German "Dorf-Assi", but with more charm and way less shame.

Stuart, as if trying to set the gold standard for bogans, pulled out a used gumboot, calmly poured a solid amount of beer into it, and downed the lot in one go. From a bloody boot! Nati and I just looked at each other — speechless. Stunned. We had tears streaming down our faces, clutched our stomachs, doubled over with laughter and were gasping for air. I genuinely thought I was going to fall off the back of the truck. Meanwhile, Stuart stood there like a king. Proud, as if he'd just broken a world record. Which, depending on how you look at it, he probably had. But the girls weren't far behind. After every drink came a burp so loud, it probably sent a few koalas flying out of the trees somewhere in Queensland. It sounded like a lost lawnmower tearing its way through the bush in the middle of the night. For us Germans, who politely clink glasses and say "cheers" with a nod, this was an actual culture shock. A loud one. A weird one. But absolutely unforgettable.

We rang in the new year — barefoot, with dirty feet, sore cheeks from laughing, and hearts full of gratitude.

That night was wild, noisy, chaotic, and somehow the perfect symbol of what 2019 had been for us: unpredictable, free, and bursting with life. Everything we'd experienced in those past few months... it's hard to put into words. Australia had changed us. It had shown us how light happiness can feel when you wake up with sunlight on your face, when there are no expectations to meet, and you're simply allowed to be yourself. This country had done something to us. It was as if it had washed away layers of insecurity, pressure, and old baggage.

No wonder so many Aussies seem to drift through life so laid-back. They grew up here, in a world that somehow feels lighter with every breath you take. Maybe some of them don't even realise what a gift surrounds them every single day. But we did. Perhaps because we knew the difference. We had let go of everything we'd clung to for years and instead placed our faith in a dream. And now here we were, standing under a starry sky in the middle of nowhere, looking at each other, laughing — and knowing one thing for sure: We hadn't regretted a single thing. This year had given us so much, and the next one was going to be even better.

# CHAPTER TWELVE
## A VISIT FROM HOME

I don't even know where to begin. So much had happened over the past few days – so many emotions, so many changes.

But before Eric finally came to visit us, something important happened: Nati and I moved out. Living with Mark's acquaintance had become increasingly difficult. Her alcohol problem was becoming more obvious by the day, and coming home after a long day of work hadn't felt like coming home for quite a while. The tiny, stuffy room we shared didn't make things any easier. We knew we couldn't go on like this.

And then, as so often happens in Australia, life itself stepped in to help. Hannah and Bob – Claire's friends, knew a woman named Roanne, an older lady from the little town of Allora.

Roanne's house was spacious and cosy, surrounded by a wide veranda where you could sit in the evenings and soak up the peaceful stillness. No noise, no rush, just birdsong and the warm breeze rustling through the trees. I loved it. That street. That house. That calm.

Roanne lived alone and was looking for a bit of company. She had heard about our difficult living situation through Hannah and Bob and immediately offered us a room. $180 per week. We agreed without hesitation. What followed was more than just a move, it was a sense of arrival. Roanne quickly became like a grandmother to us.

She was often out and about, trusted us with her home, and cooked for us with the kind of warm, effortless care you usually only know from childhood. For us, it was a small new beginning. A real home. At last.

The only bitter note: Summer, the little dog from our old place. We had grown so attached to her, the way she greeted us with pure joy when we came home, the way she looked at us when we picked up the leash. But we had to leave her behind. We knew she wasn't getting the life she deserved there. But there was nothing we could do. Life had to move on.

Work was going well, we finally had routine, a home, some structure. And then came the message we'd all been waiting for: Eric was coming. Finally! After more than half a year apart, after weeks of planning, anticipation, and longing, Nati would finally get to hug her Eric again.

We had everything ready: three weeks of road-tripping, a proper holiday. A break from work. My birthday was coming up too. And all we wanted was to live. Nati was nervous. Excited. I could see it in her face. Eric was counting the days, the hours, probably even the minutes. And me? I was just so happy. For her. For us. For everything ahead of us. The next few weeks would change everything. They were bound to become one of the highlights of our entire journey, and we were ready for it!

Nati and I were full of excitement – our big road trip was finally about to begin! Three weeks in which we just wanted to enjoy life. Three weeks of going with the flow, sun on our faces, wind in our hair, and freedom in our hearts.

Before we could set off, our trusty car had to be road-ready. We packed everything carefully: bikinis, our GoPro, sunscreen, hiking boots, emergency meds, sun hats, charging cables, snacks, power banks, a small travel cooler, sleeping bags, hammocks, headlamps – everything you'd need for a proper Aussie road trip. We did one last load of laundry, because one thing was certain: over the next few weeks, washing machines would be a rare luxury. Once everything was packed, all that was left was excitement. That tingling, almost childlike excitement that bubbles up before an adventure.

We hit the road early in the morning, heading towards Brisbane – about a three-hour drive from Allora. We had booked ourselves into a hostel for two or three nights. Nati and Eric would have a private room to themselves, and I treated myself to my own little space as well. We wanted to enjoy the first few days in peace – no stress, no plans, just time to arrive and settle in. Eric's flight was due to land around 8pm.

Nati and I spent the day leisurely wandering through the city, walking the streets, grabbing coffees, browsing the shops – but inside, we were counting down the minutes until we could finally wrap him in our arms again.

Then we got the call from Eric. He was stranded in Sydney! His flight from Europe had been delayed, and even though he gave it everything he had, sprinting like a madman from gate to gate, he missed his connecting flight to Brisbane. The Sydney Airport – which is more like a small city than a regular airport, made it impossible to get anywhere quickly. Now he was stuck there, alone, exhausted, hungry, in a nearly deserted terminal. The gates were closed, the last flight gone, the lights dimmed. No accommodation, no food, no water. No next flight until the morning. To top it all off, he hadn't been served any food or drinks on his 20+ hour flight with Scoot. There was nothing we could do. Absolutely nothing.

We had looked forward to this moment so much – the reunion, the hug, the laughter, that feeling of coming back together after so long apart.

But then, the next morning, the redeeming message came:
»I'm at the gate. I'm on my way«

We rushed to Brisbane Airport, hearts pounding, eyes already a little teary. He was finally here. As soon as Eric stepped out of the terminal, Nati ran to him and threw her arms around him in pure joy. Tears were flowing – this time, happy ones. I stood a few steps away, watching the scene with glassy eyes and a wide smile on my face. It was one of those moments where you're just deeply grateful to have everyone together again.

Back at the hostel, we dropped our bags, took a quick shower, caught our breath, and headed straight back out into the city.

Our first stop: Eggs Benedict – our absolute favourite dish in Australia. And as we sat there, we felt it clearly:

*»our road trip had finally begun.«*

# CHAPTER THIRTEEN
## K'GARI

After a few eventful days in Brisbane, during which we showed Eric around the city, we packed our things and headed off to Hervey Bay.

The drive from Brisbane took about three to four hours. Our destination: K'gari, better known as Fraser Island – the largest sand island in the world. K'gari is a true natural paradise and is part of the UNESCO World Heritage. The island is known for its breathtaking landscape: crystal-clear freshwater lakes like the famous Lake McKenzie, endless sandy beaches, dense rainforests and impressive sand dunes. One of the most popular spots is 75 Mile Beach, which serves not only as a beach but also as an official highway. Tourists are drawn to K'gari for its unique flora and fauna, the chance to see wild dingoes in their natural habitat, and the many adventures the island offers.

To get there, we booked a ferry online from River Heads to Wanggoolba Creek. The ferry crossing took around 40 minutes and cost between 165 and 175 AUD per vehicle, depending on the season. In addition, we needed a Vehicle Access Permit, which had to be purchased online beforehand. Before boarding the ferry, we stopped at a petrol station to fill up the tank. There are only a few places to refuel on K'gari – in Eurong, Happy Valley, and Kingfisher Bay, and fuel prices are significantly higher than on the mainland. So it's definitely a good idea to fill up before heading over. Before driving the car onto the ferry, we let some air out of the tyres to improve traction on the sand. We also stocked up on supplies for the next few days, as shopping options on the island are limited.

We had already booked our campsites online in advance, as they fill up quickly, especially during peak season. Wild camping is not allowed on K'gari, all camping spots must be reserved ahead of time.

The moment we finally arrived on K'gari and our tyres touched the white sand was indescribable.

We drove straight along the beach – to our left, dense, green bushland; to our right, the endless blue sea. The wind swept through the open windows, the sun warmed our faces, and the sound of crashing waves was our constant companion. It felt like pure freedom, like driving through an untouched paradise, far away from civilisation. Every kilometre on this island felt like the start of a new adventure, and we could hardly wait to explore all the wonders K'gari had to offer.

As soon as we left the mainland behind and our tyres touched the fine sand of K'gari, it felt like we had entered another world. A world of white, blue, and lush green. An island that felt like a natural wonder just waiting to be discovered.

Driving along 75 Mile Beach was an adventure in itself. Where else in the world do you get to drive a 4WD directly on the beach, with the glittering ocean to your right and a dense, almost tropical-looking forest rushing past on your left?

Our first stop was the famous Lake McKenzie, an absolute dream. Crystal-clear, turquoise water surrounded by the finest white silica sand. It felt like swimming in a giant infinity pool crafted by Mother Nature herself. The water was soft on the skin, and the sand so fine it almost crunched like powdered sugar beneath our feet. We spent hours there, swimming, laughing, taking photos, and simply letting our souls breathe.

Over the next few days, we explored everything the island had to offer: the Maheno Shipwreck, the rusty skeleton of an old ship lying in the middle of the beach, as if it had stood there for centuries, silently telling its story.

The Champagne Pools were another highlight – natural rock pools by the sea, where every crashing wave creates fizzy bubbles on your skin, like sparkling water.

Then there was Eli Creek, a crystal-clear stream flowing gently over the sand, shallow enough to lie in and float along with the current. And Indian Head, with its breathtaking views over the ocean – a spot where you might even spot dolphins, turtles, or sharks.

We spent our nights at an official campsite nestled in the dunes, surrounded by nature. Campfires were off-limits due to the high risk of bushfires at that time of year.

We didn't have any human neighbours, but we did have some regular animal visitors – most notably, a pretty impressive sand goanna. These large lizards are often mistaken for Komodo dragons, though they aren't actually related. But this one clearly felt right at home with us, regularly stopping by in search of something to eat. Even though our rubbish bag was tightly sealed, the smell must've been too tempting to resist. Morning and evening, he'd sneak up. Silently. Sometimes it seemed like the sand itself had moved, and suddenly, there he was. Staring, with his long forked tongue, steady gaze, and strong claws. I kind of liked him. There was something ancient about him. Like a dinosaur. Calm, grounded, and... present.

Although sand goannas aren't aggressive, they still deserve respect. They're wild animals, and if they feel threatened, they can bite. Their bites aren't deadly, but they are painful, and, like many reptiles, they carry bacteria that can cause serious infections.

One evening, Nati and I had just set out to take a quick sunset photo at the beach. The light was golden, the air still, with nothing but the soft sound of the waves in the background – until suddenly, right at our feet, a black snake slithered across the white sand. Fast, sleek, and elegant. And extremely venomous. We froze. I felt my heart pounding in my throat. Then, at the exact same time, we both leapt backwards in a perfectly synchronised panic move. The snake continued on, completely unfazed by our shock.

Later, we found out it was most likely an Eastern Small-eyed Snake, one of Australia's most venomous species. Its bite can paralyse the nervous system within minutes and requires immediate medical attention. So yeah… the sunset was definitely cancelled after that. Instead, we headed back to our "accommodation," drank a glass of water, and took a few deep breaths.

During that time, our tent had become our little safe haven. In fact, we only had one large tent, so the three of us shared it – let's call it cosy… in the most affectionate sense of the word.

Nati and Eric had absolutely no privacy, of course, because their little "travel tag-along" (yep, me) lay right in the middle every night like a kid who got to come along on a school trip. They just had to deal with it.

The only thing missing was a guitar to make the picture complete — though, honestly, even if we'd had one, none of us would've known how to play it. We probably would've driven the entire campground away with our "talents" rather than entertained them… But honestly, it was perfect just the way it was. Three people, one tent, one island, and unforgettable moments. Nothing else needed.

But K'gari had one more big test in store for us. Because there's one piece of advice that comes up again and again when you're planning a trip to Fraser Island:

*»Whatever you do, take a spare tyre!«*


Well. Guess what we didn't do. Right in the middle of the island, somewhere along the endless beach, not a soul in sight, no houses, no phone reception — we suddenly heard a suspicious noise. A hissing. Then a wobble. Then… Bam.

Our tyre had completely blown out. Not just a little tear that you could maybe patch up. No, the rubber was torn from front to back like an exploding sausage. Beyond repair. Total write-off. Sand: 1 – Tyre: 0.

And as if that wasn't stressful enough, those bloody little flies showed up again. The same pests that had nearly eaten us alive at Uluru. They were everywhere: in our faces, in our ears, under our clothes, on our scalps. Every pore on our bodies became a target. And really, we had better things to do than act as insect bodyguards.

But what choice did we have? Phone reception? None. Help? Not a soul in sight. We had no option but to leave the car behind on the beach, which was a real risk — the tides change fast around here. But we had no other choice. So off we trudged. Through the hot, soft sand. For several kilometres. Sweaty, bitten, frustrated, but somehow also laughing, because we knew: If we survived this, we'd have one hell of a story to tell.

After nearly an hour of walking, we finally reached a small information centre. Relief. Hope. We ran up to the door… and of course, it was closed. It was Sunday! A little sign hung outside:

*»Open Monday to Friday.«*


Just great. But at least there were a few phone numbers pinned up. We clung to the hope that someone — anyone, might actually pick up. So we grabbed the phone, walked a little further until we finally had reception, and started calling every number we could find – like playing the lottery. And unbelievably, someone actually picked up.

A friendly man calmly explained that we should keep

walking a bit further. After a few more steps through the hot sand, we came across a tiny settlement right in the middle of Fraser Island. We had no idea people even lived out there, but there were indeed a few scattered houses – and more importantly: people! We knocked on a few doors, explained our situation for what felt like the twentieth time, and finally got lucky. An older man, tanned by the sun and grinning from ear to ear, just said:

»Sure, I can help you out. I've got a spare tyre. Hop in.«

He drove us in his rusty pickup truck back to the beach, where our poor car was still standing, thankfully not already half underwater. The tide had definitely crept closer, and we really weren't far off from turning our road trip into a boat trip. The man swapped the tyre in no time, chuckled at our story, and only asked for 50 dollars. No rip-off, no hassle, just a kind-hearted, easy-going local who helped us out when we needed it the most. He'd probably rescued hundreds of backpackers who thought they didn't need a spare tyre. We weren't the first, but thanks to him, we weren't lost either.

That evening, back at our campsite, we collapsed onto our mattresses half dead. Exhausted, covered in bites, sweaty – but happy. We couldn't stop laughing about the whole "funny" event, which in hindsight was just too ridiculous to be annoyed about.

K'gari had challenged us, surprised us, and in the end, deeply impressed us. This island is wild, beautiful, and unforgettable.

The next morning, it was time to say goodbye, with one laughing eye and one crying.

We carefully packed up all our chaos again, rolled up the sleeping bags, stowed away the tent and all our gear in the car, and made our way back to the ferry. Once more, the white sand lay beneath our tyres, as if to let us feel again where we had lived, sweated, laughed, and learned over the past few days.

Then we left K'gari, grateful, tired, and full of impressions. Back to the mainland, and on to the next adventure!

As the ferry slowly turned away, we took one last look at the island. The outline of K'gari faded into the salty spray as we silently waved our farewell, just like you do with an old friend you're being forced to let go of far too soon.

At the same time, a new sense of anticipation began to stir within us: for the mainland, for new impressions, and unexpected experiences. Right after arriving at Inskip Point, we spontaneously decided to turn right and drive down a quiet, remote stretch of coastline, where the sand still gave way softly under the tyres, and the ocean shimmered in a deep blue. As we set foot on the mainland again, there was that comforting calm in the air — the kind you only really notice when a crossing has gone well. We felt relaxed, yet full of excitement for whatever was still to come.

The day wasn't over yet, and we could feel it. No sooner had we parked the car than we saw something out on the water from a distance. A movement, hard to place. We jumped out of the car, barefoot into the still-warm sand, looked at each other, and then ran. So excited, like children who've just discovered something magical they can't afford to miss. We laughed, shouted over each other, pointed towards the sea and almost tripped over ourselves in our rush. Something was moving in the water. At first, just a dark shadow beneath the surface, then a shiny back broke through the light. A dolphin! Just seconds later, a second appeared. Then another. And suddenly they were there, a small pod, right near the shore. So close that I instinctively reached my hand into the water, as if I could actually touch them. One of the dolphins swam straight towards us—graceful, curious, almost playful. They spun around each other, dove down together, resurfaced, gliding closely side by side as if teasing one another. You could feel how familiar they were with each other. It almost seemed like they were inviting us into their little world, just for a few minutes.

We stood in the shallow water, barefoot, damp from the ocean spray, grinning from ear to ear. I can't even count how many times we shouted,

*»Oh my god!«* or
*»Did you see that?!«*

It's in moments like these that you realise just how lucky you are. That you get to stand in a place like this, with the sea in front of you, real dolphins right there, and the freedom to witness all of it with your own eyes.

Eventually, they slowly moved on, disappearing one by one into the open water again. We stayed for a moment longer, watching them go, barely able to believe what had just happened. With hearts bursting with joy, we got back in the car and drove on towards Rainbow Beach.

We had booked a small hostel for the night, but deep down, we already knew: the most beautiful moment of the day was already behind us.

Once we arrived, we treated ourselves to a well-deserved break. Pizza, Coke, and a bit of laughter. The air was still warm, the salt clung to our clothes, and our minds were buzzing with memories. We talked about the past few days, retelling the same stories to each other, even though we had experienced them all together — just to relive them once more.

Later, when we finally crawled into our beds with tired limbs, sandy feet and full hearts, we were all thinking the same thing, even if no one said it out loud:

*»How could anything ever top this?«*

# CHAPTER FOURTEEN

## SUNSHINE & SURFING

It was Eric's last two weeks with us in Australia, and we wanted to make the most of them. But before moving on, we treated ourselves to two more relaxing, yet adventure-filled days in Rainbow Beach. This rugged, wind-swept coastline had fascinated us from the moment we arrived – brightly coloured sand cliffs, an endlessly wide horizon, and the untamed ocean stretching out before us.

We drove our 4WD along the beach, salty water spraying up to the side mirrors, the wind tugging at our hair, and our faces stretched in constant grins.

On one of those days, Eric and I grabbed my surfboard and hit the water. I really wanted to show him a few basics – how to paddle, when to pop up, how to read the wave. And honestly, it was going pretty well. At least until an unexpectedly strong wave rolled in, and my board suddenly turned against me. I dove under, lost control of the board for a split second, and that's when the fin caught me right on the forehead. It wasn't a deep cut, but enough to leave a proper bump and a bit of blood. We immediately got out of the water. Eric looked at me, concerned, and asked if I was okay. The shock was real – for both of us. Thankfully, it wasn't anything serious. Still, my head throbbed all day, and the headache stuck around. That was the end of surfing for the day. Once again, I was reminded that the ocean isn't always a playground.

The next day, we continued our trip, but not without a stop that had us laughing nonstop – the Aqua Park Coolum. A giant inflatable water park floating on a lake, with slides, climbing walls and obstacles that sent us flying through the air like kids – or, more often, crashing into the water in the most spectacular fashion. It was one of those days where you already feel the soreness coming, but you don't care, because your stomach already hurts from laughing so much.

Afterward, we made our way towards the Sunshine Coast, but with a little detour. We wanted to take the scenic route, the same one Nati and I had fallen in love with during our first trip through the area: past the majestic Glass House Mountains.

These dark, almost mystical volcanic peaks stood like ancient guardians scattered across the landscape, nestled among lush green fields, palm trees, and little farmhouses.

By early evening, we were hungry and decided to treat

ourselves to a proper meal.

What we found wasn't just "nice", it turned out to be one of the absolute highlights of our journey: the Hinterland Restaurant. Tucked away in a tropical-looking stretch of hinterland, surrounded by eucalyptus trees and fluttering lanterns on the veranda, this stylish little gem looked like something straight out of an interior design magazine. Warm lights, muted colours, soft music.

We sat out on the terrace, watching the sunset glimmer through the treetops, barely able to believe how good food could taste when it's made with real love. Definitely not your typical backpacker dinner. It was pricier than usual, yes, but worth every dollar. To this day, I'd rank it as one of my all-time top restaurant experiences.

After our evening at the Hinterland Restaurant, where everything had felt so perfect, we climbed back into our Goldi – full, content, and a little enchanted.

By now, it was pitch-black outside. The surrounding trees cast dark shadows, and only the restaurant lanterns flickered softly through the window as we closed the door behind us. Our next destination: Noosa, right at the top of the Sunshine Coast. The drive took about an hour, a quiet journey through the night-time hinterland, along winding country roads that rolled through gentle hills. Outside, you could barely see anything, just the occasional flash of headlights or a kangaroo darting across the road at the edge of your vision.

Unlike usual, we hadn't booked a hostel this time but found a room through Airbnb — the three of us: Eric, Nati, and I. At first glance, everything seemed harmless: a modern house, clean, quietly located, not particularly charming but perfectly fine for one night. The owner greeted us kindly at the door, her husband stood a little further back in the hallway. Both were clearly older, perhaps in their early seventies, and in their own way... unusual. Not unfriendly. Just somehow odd.

»*I'm a psychologist*«,

she said with a proud smile that didn't quite match her piercing eyes. We followed her up the stairs to our room, and by the time we got there, we knew something wasn't quite right. All along the way were porcelain dolls. On window sills, in little wooden shelves, on a wobbly side table. These things stared at us like something out of a bad horror film — silent, pale, lifeless. Then there was the hallway, its walls painted in wild colours. Not cheerful and bright, but... chaotic. As if someone had spilled their entire emotional life onto the walls with a paintbrush. I felt like I was trapped in a nightmare I might wake up from... or not. We looked at each other but didn't say anything at first. Maybe we were overreacting. Maybe this was just a quirky old lady with a creative flair for interior design. But the moment we got into our room, we said it out loud: This place was creepy. Properly creepy.

That night we heard noises, footsteps, muffled voices, creaking in the hallway. Probably harmless. Still, Eric and I put a few things on the door handle, just in case someone tried to come in. I think we even placed a couple of pins or a bottle cap in front of the door. Totally ridiculous, but somehow it made us feel better to be prepared. The atmosphere reminded me of one of those films where nothing actually happens, but you just know the whole time that something's off.

The next morning they wanted to have breakfast with us. We thanked them politely, quickly packed our things, and said goodbye with the friendliest smiles we could manage. When we closed the door behind us and started the car, there was only one thought in our minds: Hopefully never again. Maybe we had overreacted. Maybe it was just an elderly couple with… let's say, interesting quirks. But one thing was certain: Our gut feeling had sounded the alarm, and sometimes, that's exactly what you need to listen to.

Afterwards, we headed to one of the small cafés in the centre of Noosa. This charming, laid-back place with a touch of luxury and surfer vibes had captivated us instantly.

We had breakfast outside on a little terrace, surrounded by palm trees, birdsong, and the gentle clinking of cutlery. The croissants were buttery, the coffee strong, life was good.

Energised, we set off towards Noosa Heads, one of the most beautiful natural spots along the entire East Coast. Noosa National Park welcomed us with its wild charm: dense eucalyptus forests, rocky cliffs, hidden coves, and turquoise sea. As we walked along the narrow coastal trail, our gaze drifting over the endless ocean, Eric suddenly spotted something in one of the tall trees. A small grey fluff ball sat curled up like a sleepyhead on a branch. A real koala. Eric's face lit up with joy.

»*Oh my god, there's one! A real one!*«.

He was absolutely thrilled, and we shared in his excitement because once again, this was one of those little wonders Australia casually gifts you.

After our relaxed day in Noosa, we couldn't resist feeling the waves one more time. The sun was hanging low in the sky, golden rays reflecting on the water as we returned to the beach with our boards under our arms. The ocean was calm, yet full of life. We laughed, rode the waves, collected shells with salty hands and took photos that would last forever. No plans, no clock – just the moment, the sun on our skin and the sand beneath our feet.

The next morning, we woke up early. Before the sun climbed high into the sky, we made our way to a place that almost felt magical: the Fairy Pools in Noosa.

The Fairy Pools are natural rock pools, hidden between the cliffs along the picturesque Coastal Track in Noosa National Park. Crystal-clear water collects there at high tide in small, sheltered basins where you can swim as if it were a secret spot made only for those truly willing to find it.

The way there was already a little adventure: from the entrance of the national park, we walked along the narrow path hugging the coast. To our right, the sea thundered against the rocks; to the left, eucalyptus trees shimmered in the morning sun. The track led past small bays, enchanted viewpoints, and finally, if you paid close attention, to a subtle turnoff that led over rocks and down to the pools. You have to do a bit of climbing, carefully feel your way over the smooth stones – and then, suddenly, the view opens up to these little natural wonders: two crystal-clear rock pools, framed by dark volcanic rock that has been smoothed over thousands of years by the salty sea. The water shimmered a turquoise green, gently trickling over the edge back into the ocean.

We took off our clothes, slid into the cool pool, and were simply happy. We had the place to ourselves. No noise, no crowds, just us, the sea, and that feeling of being exactly where we were meant to be.

The next morning wasn't just any day, it was my birthday. Another year older, still far from home, and yet, not alone. No family around me, no cake from Mum, no hug from Dad. But instead: Nati and Eric. My little temporary family. And the two of them made this day one of those special kinds.

I was still lying under the thin blanket in our hostel bed, while the first rays of sun snuck through the curtains outside. What I didn't know: the two of them had already been up for a while. And that, even though they're both definitely not early birds – quite the opposite. But that morning, they got up earlier than ever, tiptoed out of the room, and headed off to the nearest supermarket.

A few days earlier, I had casually mentioned that there was only one thing I really wanted for my birthday: a soft, fluffy brioche bun with a thick layer of Nutella. Nothing else. Just a small taste of home.

When I finally got up, still sleepy and with messy hair—I

walked into the little shared kitchen of the hostel, and there it was: a breakfast table, set just for me. Plates, cups, warm brioche, Nutella, fresh fruit. Two beaming faces looked up at me.

*»Happy Birthday«,*

they whispered. And I knew: there was nowhere else in the world I would have rather woken up than right here. The day had only just begun, and it already had a smile on my face. But we also knew: we didn't have much time, because a very special adventure still lay ahead.

We had booked a ferry trip to Moreton Island, an island located just about 40 kilometres off the coast of Brisbane, yet it feels like an entirely different world.

Moreton Island, or "Mulgumpin" as it's known in the language of the Quandamooka Aboriginal people, is the third-largest sand island in the world. It's known for its untouched nature, golden dunes, crystal-clear waters and the famous "Tangalooma Wrecks."

These wrecks are fifteen sunken ships that were deliberately placed there in the 1960s to create a safe anchorage for boats. Today, they're a paradise for divers and snorkellers. Between rusted steel skeletons slowly covered in coral, hundreds of fish swim about, sometimes turtles, and if you're lucky—even dolphins.

We caught the ferry from Brisbane. The crossing took about 75 minutes. The ride alone was an experience: the sparkling ocean, wind in our hair, and that view straight ahead—towards adventure. When we reached the island, it felt like we'd landed in a movie. White sand as far as the eye could see. Palm trees swaying gently in the breeze. No cars, no noise. Just nature. And in the middle of it all: the three of us. With our dive gear, full of excitement, ready to dive in—literally and figuratively.

We made our way to our dive guide, who greeted us with a wide grin. The sun was high in the sky, and the water was as clear as glass. Perfect conditions for our first shared diving adventure. Before heading out on the boat, the day started with a short practice session for everyone joining the dive. In a pool, we were walked through the basics again—skills that could mean the difference between safety and danger underwater.

*»How do you breathe properly through the regulator? How do you equalise the pressure in your ears? What do you do if water gets in your mask or you lose your mouthpiece? How do you signal a problem underwater, and why must you never, ever hold your breath while surfacing?«*

Diving is magical, but it requires focus and respect. One wrong move, one ascent too fast, and your body reacts with dizziness, panic, or even injury. That's why everything was explained calmly and systematically. No pressure, no stress. Just breath by breath – the way it should be later in the depths as well.

Nati and I still remembered a lot from before. We had already done a dive at the Great Barrier Reef, our very first one. Back then, we went down about seven metres. But today, we would be diving to depths of up to 13 metres. And that's a difference you can feel. The deeper you descend, the more the world changes. The light begins to fade. Everything gets darker, cooler, quieter. Colours vanish. All that's left is blue, green, shadows. Your own breathing becomes the only sound, a steady companion in a foreign world.

I never thought my love for the ocean and the depths could grow even more, but that's exactly what happened. The silence, the weightlessness, the depth. Something inside me became incredibly calm down there – calmer than I had ever felt before. I felt free. Centred. Grounded. It was almost like an addiction, and I could've stayed there for hours. In that underwater world, where time seemed to stand still. All around us, the massive, rusting shipwrecks rose from the sand. They looked like sunken temples, reclaimed by nature, covered in coral, moss, barnacles. In between: life. Everywhere. Schools of tiny, shimmering silver fish glided past us like glittering veils. A few curious clownfish were hiding in vibrant anemones. Fish nibbled on the algae. Further back, a small reef shark glided past, graceful and unimpressed by our presence. Among the wreckage, we spotted stingrays, sea urchins, and even a majestic turtle slowly drifting over the ocean floor. The colours were muted, not postcard-perfect like when snorkelling, but subdued turquoise, smoky blue, rusty red.

But as magical as this dive was, there came a moment that reminded us all just how quickly things can shift underwater.

We'd been down there for a while when it happened. I'm not exactly sure how. Maybe it was the silence down there, the weightless gliding through the water, the play of light between the wrecks. Maybe I was just enjoying the moment a little too much. Whatever it was, at some point, I drifted too far away from the group. Eric told me later that he had seen me, how I floated ahead through the water, completely lost in my own world, not looking back once, not caring where the rest of the group was. He said I didn't care about the guide, or the others—just me and my little underwater paradise.

Honestly, I barely remember it myself. I must have really been in my own bubble. I probably wouldn't have noticed being completely alone until half an hour later, and then calmly thought:

»Well, alright, maybe I should slowly surface. My oxygen's almost gone anyway«.

But for Eric, it was anything but calm. He had long noticed that I'd lost connection with the group and that I wasn't even trying to return in my Zen bubble. So, he picked up the pace, swam toward me as quickly as possible, constantly scanning for my fins. When he finally reached me, he made it crystal clear, with eyes and hand signals: Back. To the group. Now. I remember looking at him, taking a moment to realise what was going on. And then it hit me, I had truly drifted off.

Together, we swam back and found Nati near a rope leading to the surface. We decided to ascend—slowly, step by step, just as we'd been taught. Equalising pressure, staying controlled, staying focused. No panic.

But once we surfaced, it was Eric who suddenly wasn't doing well. The whole commotion underwater, the fast swimming, the increased air consumption – all of it had taken a toll on him. Even as we removed our gear, he started feeling nauseous. Every step on the boat seemed like a struggle. I felt awful. Not just because of my little solo dive, but because I was once again reminded how quickly things can change underwater, and how important it is to keep an eye on one another. Even if you're totally mesmerised by a rusty propeller.

But what exactly had happened? A lot of things can come together when diving, and even if you do everything "right", sometimes the body reacts differently. Stress underwater can affect your breathing rate. If you start breathing more shallowly, you exhale less $CO_2$, which can lead to what's known as $CO_2$ retention – causing dizziness, nausea, and headaches. A rapid ascent, even with a rope, can result in what's called "barotrauma" – irritation in the lungs, sinuses or inner ear. And sometimes, sheer panic is enough to throw the body completely off balance, especially underwater, where everything is delayed.

Eric was lucky. He didn't lose consciousness. His eardrum didn't rupture. No signs of decompression sickness. But his body had made it crystal clear: it was too much. We needed a break. Desperately.

Back on land, we let the day wind down slowly. We spread out our towels under the palm trees by the beach, lay in the shade, and let our eyes wander across the calm sea. The sand was warm, the light golden. Eric fell asleep. Nati and I lay beside him, each lost in our own thoughts. After about two hours, he was back on his feet—still a little pale, but himself again. And even though that moment had shaken us, it didn't leave behind fear. Instead, it left a new sense of respect for the ocean. A quiet knowing: this isn't our element. But if we enter it with humility, it can give us the greatest gifts.

In the late afternoon, we took the ferry back to the mainland. The sun hung low, the water sparkled, and even though the day had been full of experiences—my birthday was far from over.

That evening, we continued our drive to Brisbane. We had something planned there that Nati and I had secretly been looking forward to for days: dinner at a German restaurant. It had been seven months since we'd last had proper German food on our plates, and just the thought of red cabbage, gravy, and dumplings made our hearts beat faster. When we arrived, a beautifully set table was already waiting for us. Nati excitedly ordered goulash, Eric went for kassler, and I—true to tradition, chose Sauerbraten. And what can I say? It was honestly really good! Almost like home. The sauces, the meat, even the red cabbage, everything was spot on. Well… except for Nati's goulash. Or, as we later said with a laugh:

»*That was everything—just not goulash*«.

But even that couldn't dampen our mood. Quite the opposite, really—it just made the evening that bit funnier.

Later, we booked a small room in a hostel. No luxury, no décor, no birthday cake. Just three backpacks, a simple room, and the constant creaking of the mattress whenever someone moved. But it was exactly what I had wished for: a day full of moments, sun, sea, adventure, and the two people who had shared all of it with me.

We sat together for a long time that night, barefoot, hair still wet from the sea, wearing comfy clothes. Somewhere, music played faintly through the walls. We laughed, talked, chatted about the dive, about home, about Australia, about what had been, and what was still to come. Everything felt light. There was no plan, no obligation, no need. Just this moment. Eventually, things got quieter. The conversations faded, our eyes grew heavier. I turned to my side, pulled the thin hostel sheet up to my chin and couldn't help but smile. It wasn't perfect in the classic sense, but it was my perfect day. My birthday. Down Under. With my two best friends.

# CHAPTER FIFTEEN
GOLD COAST & GOODBYE

We still had one week left with Eric, and we wanted to make the most of it, right up to the very last day.
Our first destination: the Cedar Creek Falls. Beforehand, we made a quick stop at Kmart, where we stocked up on brightly coloured inflatable swim rings. We'd read that you could float right beneath the waterfall in the cool water – a mental image that had taken root in our minds. And just like we had imagined, it was absolutely magical.

The drive from Brisbane to the falls took less than an hour. As soon as we parked the car, a short enchanted trail led us through lush greenery. It smelled of damp eucalyptus, of stones warmed by the sun, and somewhere in the distance we could already hear the sound of rushing water. Then we saw it: rocks surrounding a turquoise-coloured pool. We threw our floaties into the water, jumped in after them, and let ourselves drift. Eric laughed, while Nati and I tried to push each other beneath the gushing water. Happy days. But the day was far from over.

A bit further down the path, we discovered what looked like a natural lake, framed by rocks, with a little ledge that seemed made for dares. A few locals were already flinging themselves into the water with fearless energy, and soon enough, we found ourselves up there too – soaked, buzzing, full of adrenaline. They climbed those steep, slippery slopes like mountain goats, while I moved like an overly cautious koala, checking each foothold at least twice to make sure it wouldn't collapse under me. When I finally reached the top, I stood there with trembling knees, staring into the depths. Nati and Eric were already in the water, floating around like it was no big deal and cheering me on with big grins. But it didn't help at all. My mind was running wild: What if I slip? What if a branch breaks? What if I bellyflop and it looks ridiculous? In short: Miss Overdramatic was having her moment again. After what felt like five years of internal debate, I finally jumped. Splash! The fear instantly turned into pure joy as I came up for air with a scream and a giant smile.

Right underneath the jumping ledge, we discovered a little rock nook, almost like a hidden cave. Quiet, shady, tucked away. No one else was there. Perfect for a quick rest – or so we thought. Just as we stretched out and started to relax, a woman paddled past, glanced over at us, and casually said, »*I wouldn't lie there if I were you... look up*«.

One glance upward was all it took to freeze us in place. Massive black spiders, bigger than our hands, were clinging to the damp ceiling above us. Their eight legs splayed out like they were lying in wait, glossy eyes fixed on us... as if we weren't guests, but prey. As if they had silently, hungrily declared us tonight's dinner. We were frozen. Then: panic mode. We jumped out of the cave and paddled back like maniacs – half laughing, half screaming, and with half a heart attack to go. What a day!

The next three days were all about sunshine, waves and big city vibes by the sea – we had arrived at the Gold Coast.

A place where the Pacific Ocean meets skyscrapers and endless sandy beaches. Even on the drive in, we were in awe. The sun reflected off the glass facades of the high-rises, while just beyond them stretched kilometres of pale sand, as if two worlds had been laid side by side: urban life and the endless sound of the sea.

The Gold Coast, located in the southeast of Queensland, is more than just a holiday spot. It's a feeling. A mix of Miami vibes, surfer paradise and laid-back Aussie spirit.

We wandered through the lively streets of Surfers Paradise, where palm trees grow beside tall towers and the salty air clings to your skin. Everything smells like sunscreen, coffee, and adventure. Iced coffee in one hand, flip-flops in the other, while your feet are already making their way back to the beach. Here, you can do it all – catch waves at the famous Main Beach breaks, go shopping in sleek malls, or sip a cocktail on a rooftop bar as the sun sinks behind the towers. We wanted to make these last few days truly special. No sightseeing marathon, no ticking off tourist spots, just creating memories. The kind of memories that settle into your soul like grains of sand.

The Gold Coast made it easy to just go with the flow – sometimes chilled, sometimes loud, sometimes wild. We treated ourselves to a massage right in the middle of Surfers Paradise, where the noise of the street seemed to fade the moment warm hands touched our tense shoulders. Afterward, everything felt a bit lighter – body, mind, and heart.

Nati and Eric wanted to spend a little time on their own too, which was totally fine with me. I'm someone who enjoys their own company, and often needs it. So I gave myself a full day of me-time: barefoot through the streets, iced coffee in hand, salt on my skin, and one wild idea in my head. Because, as life goes – a little impulse turned into a tattoo. Or... two. I was already pretty "decorated," as some might say. My body is quite covered in tattoos by now, same with Nati, by the way. We're two cute girls with a whole lot of ink. You wouldn't necessarily notice at first glance, but hey, surprise!

I got a large wave tattooed on my heel. Not your typical basic wave, but one I designed myself, a symbol for all the times the ocean had felt like home. And then I added another one: on my arm now sits a palm tree, an endless ocean, and a girl with a surfboard in hand. I already knew while it was being done that this tattoo wouldn't be the final version. But are they ever really finished?

Tattoos are like chips – no one stops at just one. Or as I always say: a beautiful, bloody expensive addiction. I ended up spending over a thousand dollars.

Eric, by the way, was finally convinced to get his first tattoo. After years of persuasion from Nati, he finally took the plunge. We went to Celebrity Ink, a well-known tattoo studio right in the heart of Surfers Paradise. Artists from all over the world work there, each with their own unique style, and you can choose exactly who you want to be inked by. Highly recommended, for anyone in the area looking for a permanent souvenir.

The day was absolutely perfect. We were tired, freshly tattooed, happy, and to top it all off, we grabbed some Ben & Jerry's ice cream. Of course, because of Nati! She's completely addicted to ice cream. I swear, if someone offered to tattoo her with an ice cream cone and three scoops, she'd say yes in a heartbeat.

After a few days, we made our way to Byron Bay. Just for a short while. A brief stop by the ocean before Eric would fly back to Germany. A little peace and quiet, one last sunset, maybe a few nice photos. Just another dot on the map. But what we didn't know was that this place had so much more in store for us. When we drove to Byron Bay with Eric, we thought it would just be the next beautiful stop on our trip. Another sunset at the beach. But Byron Bay was different. Right when we arrived, there was this feeling—hard to explain, but instantly noticeable. As if the place itself had something to say. As if the waves, the palm trees, the music, the people, the air here… were different.

We only spent two days there with Eric, who would soon return to Germany. It was a beautiful, carefree time. We wandered barefoot through the little streets, laughed in cafés, watched the surfers dancing on the waves, and felt every minute: Here, you're allowed to simply be. No masks, no roles. Free.

What we didn't know at the time: Byron Bay wouldn't let us go that easily. It wasn't just a stop on our route, it was a chapter that hadn't finished writing itself. A chapter that, much later, without warning, would turn our lives upside down. Because nearly two months later, completely unexpectedly, Nati and I would return here. And this place would feel like home. Not just on a map, but in our souls. Byron Bay changed me. Not at first glance, but little by little. My thoughts, my values, my view of life—and eventually, even my future.

But we didn't know any of that back then. We were still just three friends on a road trip, at the end of a long day, with our feet in the sand, our hearts full of sea air, and our heads in the clouds. Just a few days that felt like the blink of an eye, yet they marked the first step into something much bigger. After those magical days in Byron Bay—days that burned into our hearts like sunsets over endless beaches, we wanted to show Eric just a little more of our life before he returned to Germany. One final mini road trip. A final adventure for the three of us.

Early in the morning, still tired from packing, we left the hostel and made our way back towards Toowoomba – the next big town and the place Nati and I had called home over the past weeks. Back to where work and responsibilities were already waiting. But not just yet. Eric was still with us.

We were still complete.

Before introducing him to our little Outback family, we took him to one of our favourite places: Sushi 3.5 – for us, the holy grail of sushi joints. Nothing else came close. Not in price, not in flavour, and definitely not in charm. And Eric? He was in heaven instantly. Plate after plate circled around us on the sushi train. In the end, his stack reached over 18 little dishes. We laughed and said: classic Eric. An eternal bottomless pit with a metabolism we were all jealous of.

In the afternoon we drove to Mark, our boss, and his family. Nati had talked so much about Eric in the weeks leading up to this that everyone was excited to finally meet him. The vibe was warm and welcoming, just like always. As usual, the evening ended at the Town Pub – a few drinks, a good steak, and stories floating through the air like red dust after a summer's day.

But the next morning was inevitable. We had to take Eric to the airport. The drive back to Brisbane was long, but it wasn't the distance that weighed heavy on us. It was the knowing. The moment they'd both quietly dreaded for days had come.

Goodbye. See you again? Yes, one day. But not tomorrow. Not next week.

The car was quiet. No music, no jokes. Just Nati's quiet sobbing from time to time. Eric, who never cried, turned his face silently to the side, but we saw it anyway: tears slowly running down his face, heavy and wordless. It was the kind of goodbye only two people experience who truly love each other. There weren't many words left. Just glances, a final stroke across the hand, a hesitant kiss, and then boarding. One last look over the shoulder as he walked through the glass doors. One last tear that fell, and then he was gone.

Nati was left behind. Empty. Exhausted. Shaken. The tears didn't stop for many hours. I held her. Said nothing. Because what could you say? That it gets better? That she's strong? She knew all that. And still, it was just… heartbreaking. But somewhere in all that pain, there was also something beautiful.

Because the kind of love that brings tears like this – is real. One that's worth waiting for. Worth hoping for. And worth coming back to.

# CHAPTER SIXTEEN
## COVID 19

We were standing once again where it had all begun – in front of the little house in Allora. The streets lay still, the fields shimmered in the warm late-summer light, while everything inside us was still echoing from the farewell. Eric had flown back to Germany.

That moment at the airport – his tears, Nati's trembling smile, our silent glances, had etched itself deep into our memories. But Australia didn't pause. It didn't wait for broken hearts. So we returned to what one might call everyday life – if such a thing even existed here.

Back to working for Mark and his family, surrounded once more by animals, paddocks, and the shimmering heat of Queensland. Two more months on the small family farm – somewhere between time-out and responsibility. We wanted to complete our 88 days for the second-year visa. We weren't entirely sure whether we'd ever use it, but in Australia, you quickly learn that plans are merely suggestions, and life has a habit of interfering whenever it pleases.

Over time, the workload started to ease. For us, it was a blessing, finally a chance to breathe. To think, to plan, to dream a little. And most importantly: to enjoy life.

We spent time with our colleagues, went out, laughed a lot, and even went to our very first rodeo with Bailey. A real rodeo, as if someone had brought a western movie to life. Dusty boots, clanging gates, cowboys riding bucking bulls. It was loud, wild, and fascinating. For one evening, it felt like we had stepped into a completely different world. Raw. Real. And exactly my thing.

∫⌒

But then, things changed. Something crept in that would soon turn not just our plans upside down, but the whole world.

*»Covid-19«*

At first, it was just news. A virus in China. The first cases in Europe. Empty streets in Italy. Overwhelmed hospitals. Travel warnings. My family had told me weeks earlier how this new virus was beginning to spread.

Honestly, we hadn't taken it seriously at first. We were on the other side of the world – in a small town with a few streets, a few cows, far from everything.

But that changed quickly. As Covid-19 reached Australia, everything suddenly moved at lightning speed.

First the international borders were closed, then even those within the country. Every traveller had to decide: fly home or stay? For many, that meant: abandon everything. Return flights. Panic.

For us, it meant: think. What would we even do in Germany? We had given up everything – no job, no flat, no structured life anymore. And even if we had, things weren't any better back there at the time. Quite the opposite. In Australia, we felt safe, despite everything. We had a roof over our heads, a car, some savings, and our health. So we stayed. But staying meant change.

The farm work was stopped – too risky for everyone involved. Uncertainty hung in the air like a dense fog that wouldn't lift. No one knew what would happen next. But one thing was clear: we had to act.

Roanne, the woman we had been living with, warned us that the state borders would also be closing in a few days. So, if we wanted to keep travelling, it had to be now. It was our last chance to leave Queensland and head to New South Wales before it was too late.

We packed everything – quickly, frantically, nervously. Every item had to go into the boot of our car, into Goldi, our little home on wheels. Then came the goodbyes.

Mark had organised a farewell barbecue for us. The whole family was there. It was warm, loving, and a little bittersweet.

Roanne cooked for us one last time that evening, as if we were her own children. We thanked her for everything – for this temporary home, for the warmth, for all the stories, and then we already had to hit the road.

Our destination: Byron Bay. We had no idea what awaited us. But we knew one thing: this wasn't the end yet.

The engine of our "Goldi" hummed quietly as we left the small town of Allora behind and made our way toward Byron Bay. The boot was packed to the brim – clothes, supplies, memories, and a good dose of uncertainty. We hit the road not really knowing what lay ahead. The streets were eerily quiet, almost unsettling. Everything felt like the beginning of something big. But not in an exciting way, more like the calm before the storm. Nothing felt normal anymore. Not for us. Not for Australia. Not for the world.

Even during the drive, we started getting phone calls from our families in Germany. The voices on the other end sounded worried. Uneasy. Almost panicked.

»*Are you coming back? How long do you plan to stay? What will happen if Australia locks everything down too?*«

We didn't have an answer. Just questions. Like everyone else. Because COVID-19, this strange new virus, was no longer just a newsflash from China. It had already spread across the entire globe.

A respiratory disease, first underestimated, and eventually feared like a shadow looming over every country, every city, every family. The virus attacked the lungs. For some, it was a mild case – a few days of fever, coughing, loss of taste. For others, it meant being put on a ventilator. Hospitalisation. Intensive care. Goodbyes without a final hug. People were dying. All over the world. Thousands. Then tens of thousands. Then millions. And the world held its breath.

Australia began responding. Borders were closed.

International flights cancelled. State borders shut down. If you weren't already where you wanted to be, tough luck. If you weren't fast, you were stuck. Free campsites were shut down one by one to prevent gatherings. Even at remote beaches, signs suddenly popped up saying:
»Closed due to COVID.«

Travel, which once felt so free and boundless, had become a race against time, rules, barricades, and uncertainty.

Supermarkets were emptied. Toilet paper – the absurd symbol of this pandemic, suddenly became more valuable than gold. People were stockpiling pasta, canned goods, hand sanitiser, and queues stretched outside pharmacies. Masks became mandatory. The world was in a state of emergency. Everywhere. And we felt the pressure too.

While Goldi rolled steadily down the highway, our minds were racing.

*»What if we get sick? What if our families get sick? What if Australia forces us to return home? What if we end up stranded somewhere, with no money, no safety, no plan?«*

We tried to stay calm. Took deep breaths. Didn't talk about everything all the time. But the fear was there. Riding with us. In the back seat. Invisible, yet ever-present.

At the same time, the world began talking about vaccines. A glimmer of hope, but it would take months before any would be approved. And even then... many people didn't want to get vaccinated. Skepticism, conspiracy theories, uncertainty. The world was split – between hope and fear, between freedom and responsibility. In Australia, many people followed the rules. But even here, there were protests. Demonstrations. Doubt. Society was changing. And us? We were two backpackers in the wrong place at the wrong time – and yet, somehow exactly where we were meant to be. Because giving up wasn't an option. Flying home meant returning to the life we'd deliberately left behind. To a country also in crisis – but without sun, without ocean, without adventure.

So we stayed. So we kept driving. So we hoped we'd make it across the border. That Byron Bay would welcome us, with a safe place to land and a moment to breathe. And maybe, with a new beginning.

But before we finally arrived in Byron Bay, we had one more call with our families. It was important to let them know that we were going to get through this. That we'd stay strong. That they didn't need to worry, even though we knew they would anyway. We asked them to keep us updated regularly, too – how they were doing, what was changing in Germany, what new developments there were. And of course, we promised to do the same: to keep them informed, what we were doing, where we were, how we were feeling.

Nati and I quickly agreed: we'd stay in a hostel in Byron Bay for now. Just to be safe, we'd already booked a few weeks in advance, not knowing that those few weeks would turn into months. Months that changed everything. Months that became some of the best of our entire lives.

We'd saved enough money during our last few weeks on Mark's farm to breathe for a while. We had no idea how things would unfold, but Australia was our dream. A goal we'd set for ourselves, something we could almost touch, and now, it was suddenly hanging by a thread. All because of a virus that turned the world upside down.

But deep down, we both knew we weren't ready to let go. Not yet. So we made a decision. We wanted to keep going, not let it get us down. Instead of giving up, we wanted to adapt – together, one step at a time. Whatever was waiting for us, we were determined to make the best of it.

Looking back, it was this very moment that set something in motion. We didn't know it at the time, but this was the beginning of a new chapter. One that would challenge us, but also make us stronger. One that helped us grow – on the inside, as people, as friends. Maybe it was the uncertainty itself that made us experience everything more deeply.

It became a time we'll never forget.

# CHAPTER SEVENTEEN
BYRON BAY—WHEN THE WIND CHANGED

I still remember those first few seconds as we drove into town. Everything immediately felt different—familiar, light, peaceful. It was that rare feeling that's hard to put into words: as if you were arriving at a place you'd never seen before, yet somehow thinking,

*»We could stay here forever.«*

Byron Bay felt like home from the very first moment. Not a place you just visit, but one where you lose yourself. Or maybe, where you find yourself.

The road wound its way through gentle hills, lined with dense forests and open fields. As we neared the town, the landscape opened up, revealing a sparkling view of the azure sea in the distance. The air was filled with the scent of salt, mingling with eucalyptus and blooming wildflowers.

As we drove into Byron Bay, we were greeted by an avenue of majestic Norfolk pines lining the main road. Their tall, symmetrical silhouettes reached up into the sky, forming a natural gateway that welcomed us into this special world.

Nati and I sat at Main Beach, a blanket beneath us, the sound of the ocean in front of us, and the sun beaming on our faces. We treated ourselves to a cold drink, looked out at the sea, and raised a toast to the time ahead – to everything we didn't yet know but could feel with every fibre of our being: this was going to be something big.

Byron Bay was more than just a beautiful place with surfers, waves and palm trees. It was a feeling. An atmosphere that instantly felt like home. The vibes, the people, the lifestyle – it's hard to put into words unless you've felt it yourself. It was like stepping into a world of its own. And both of us fell in love immediately. Not just with the sunsets, the street music, the cafés, the barefoot walks and the salty air. But with the life itself. With this place, where we had arrived at exactly the right moment.

That evening, we checked into YHA Byron Bay, a modern, two-storey hostel in the heart of town, just a short walk from the beach. The hostel had a central courtyard with an inviting pool, surrounded by tropical plants and colourful murals. It wasn't a resort, but it felt like one—at the budget of a hostel. Thanks to the COVID times, prices had dropped nearly in half, barely any tourists were left in the country, and we were able to afford a private room. Two single beds, our own little oasis. No strangers in the room, no shared lockers, no loud snoring from the next bunk. Just the two of us. Peace, privacy, freedom. Exactly what we needed, exactly where we found it.

Looking back, it almost felt like fate that we were there at that time. Byron Bay is usually a place people can only afford for a few days—if at all. Prices are typically sky-high. After all, this little coastal town is one of the most popular and sought-after destinations in Australia.

Hollywood stars like Chris Hemsworth, who owns a massive estate there with his family, live here permanently. Even Zac Efron spent an extended period in Byron Bay during the pandemic, cut off from the rest of the world, in the middle of paradise.

No wonder, once you've experienced this place, you never want to leave. Under normal circumstances, it would've been nearly impossible for us to live there for so long and so freely. But the pandemic changed everything. Prices dropped, hostels were half-empty, and suddenly, life in Byron Bay became accessible even to backpackers like us. We could afford so many things that would've been unthinkable before—a private room, good food, small everyday pleasures, without constantly having to watch every dollar. It felt like the universe had paused for a moment just to open a door for us. A door into a life that felt light. Free. Right. As if everything had a deeper meaning. Destiny. It couldn't have been anything else.

Our first proper day in Byron Bay began with sunlight streaming through the white curtains, the gentle splashing of the pool outside, and this inner feeling that a very special chapter was about to begin.

We woke up in our little paradise room at the YHA—two single beds, lots of light, tropical air, and calm. Even though we had practically collapsed into bed the night before. After the long drive, the packing stress, and the hectic rush to make it across the border in time, our energy had been completely drained. We had gotten through so much that day, and at the same time, we felt like we had finally arrived. No wonder we'd gone to bed early. But that's exactly what made this morning so special: the first real awakening in Byron Bay.

We started the day full of excitement, and of course, our first stop was the supermarket. And that's when we noticed something that made us both marvel and laugh: everyone was barefoot. Not just on the beach, but literally everywhere. On the street, in cafés, even while grocery shopping. We looked at each other, shook our heads and thought: this can't be serious, right? But Byron Bay was serious. At first, it felt strange to us, barefoot in a supermarket? Unthinkable in Germany. But in Byron? Totally normal. People here live differently—more relaxed, freer, less tied to societal rules. And honestly? After a few days, it became normal for us too. Our shoes stayed in the backpack, or at the hostel altogether. It felt surprisingly good to walk the streets barefoot. Free. Light. No one looked at us weird. It was as if no one judged how you looked or what you wore. Byron Bay isn't your typical town. No concrete jungle, no filth, no chaos.

We realised that Australian towns are far cleaner than what we were used to in Germany. Less rubbish, hardly any cigarette butts, no stench. People here respect nature, and each other.

After shopping, we headed back to the hostel and were greeted with open arms in the kitchen. The atmosphere was vibrant, colourful, loud and joyful. Laughter, singing and joking echoed through the space. A delightful mix of languages: mostly Spanish, with some French, a little German, and lots of English with heavy accents. At the time, there were heaps of Spanish and Argentinian travellers living in the hostel, along with a few French ones. A mix of people from all over the world, but mostly warm-hearted, fun-loving souls from South America and Southern Europe. Everyone was open, friendly and curious. As soon as we stepped into the kitchen, we were greeted:

»*Hey, are you new here? What's your name?*«.

We instantly felt at home. Not like strangers, but like two people who belonged. Our English had already improved a lot, we could have proper conversations and even crack a few jokes. Sure, sometimes we'd forget a word and quickly look it up on our phones, but that was okay. That was part of learning. No one laughed, no one rolled their eyes. On the contrary, everyone helped each other, and that's what made it so lovely.

After a relaxed breakfast and lots of exciting conversations, we decided to explore more of Byron Bay. We packed our things, reapplied sunscreen, threw our beach towels over our shoulders and headed out—barefoot, of course, to Main Beach, our new favourite place. As we strolled through the little alleys, surrounded by palm trees, tropical plants, vegan cafés and surfers with salt in their hair,

we both thought the same thing:
*»How beautiful can life actually be?«*.

After a day spent at the beach and wandering through narrow laneways filled with vintage shops, colourful cafés and street musicians, Nati and I returned to the hostel in the evening — tired, sun-kissed, and happy.

We took showers, slipped into comfy clothes and cooked ourselves a simple but delicious dinner in the communal kitchen. The air was filled with the smell of stir-fried veggies, pasta and spices from all around the world, like a culinary backpacker concert with ingredients from a hundred different countries. After eating, we sat outside in the open common area, where long wooden tables stood beneath trees wrapped in fairy lights. And it was exactly on this evening that something happened, something that would leave a lasting mark on our time in Byron Bay.

At one of the tables sat two guys, whom I can no longer just call "acquaintances", because they became much more than that. A real part of this story. A real part of our lives.

Their names were Marzio and Nici. Two Germans, whom we saw for the very first time in that moment. They were sitting there, just as they apparently did every evening — smoking, laughing, and often deep into a game of chess. It was the kind of scene you'd expect from an old French film.

I honestly can't remember who made the first move. Maybe we asked if they were from Germany. Maybe they recognised us. It doesn't matter. It was one of those moments when you just know: this clicks.

That very night, we ended up talking for hours. About everything and nothing — travel, music, dreams, all the things that fill your head when you're far from home and suddenly meet people you instantly connect with.

From that night on, we were inseparable. Nati, me, Marzio and Nici, our own little Byron Bay quartet.

We spent countless evenings together, laughing, cooking, sitting at the beach, dreaming up future plans. Of course, there were also days where we got on each other's nerves, but even then, we knew: we belonged together, somehow.

And because I know these words might one day be read by Eric, and maybe others who wonder whether real friendship between a man and a woman can truly exist — I want to make this very clear: yes, it absolutely can. Between the four of us, there was never anything more than that. It was never complicated. It was pure. A real, deep friendship, like siblings you got to choose yourself.

Of course, Eric was a bit jealous at first, understandably so, being on the other side of the world and hearing that two guys were suddenly part of our everyday life. But not long after, even he realised there was no room for misunderstandings. We were friends. Nothing more, and nothing less.

This friendship was more than just a travel coincidence. It was something real, and it has remained to this day.

After all the laughter and late-night talks with Marzio and Nici on our first evening together, we spontaneously decided to head to the supermarket. It was already late, but we didn't want the moment to end just yet. So we bought a few bottles of wine and, slightly giddy and full of euphoria, made our way to the beach. In the middle of the night, we sat there in the sand, facing the dark ocean, a blanket beneath us, wine bottles between us, and the feeling that something was beginning – something we wouldn't easily forget.

We laughed a lot, talked about anything and everything, and yes, at some point we were all quite drunk.

Eventually, we stumbled back to the hostel, slurring, giggling, barely able to hold our toothbrushes, and then collapsed straight into bed.

The next morning, we woke up slightly hungover but full of excitement for the day. We hadn't even planned to have breakfast together, but somehow it just happened. Even though Marzio and Nici weren't exactly morning people – especially Marzio rarely made it out of bed early, and Nici was sometimes even worse – we somehow all ended up at the table together. It felt like we had always done it that way.

By the way, the boys also had a private room at the hostel. And just as you'd imagine: two guys in a tiny hostel room, it looked like a bomb had gone off. It smelled like gym shoes, socks were scattered everywhere, and it felt like stepping into the bedroom of a 16-year-old teenager. But we loved them anyway and accepted them just the way they were.

After breakfast, we decided to drive to Whites Beach – one

of Byron Bay's hidden gems. The drive took us through Broken Head Nature Reserve, about 10 kilometres south of Byron Bay. We followed Seven Mile Beach Road, then turned onto a narrow, unsealed track winding through dense subtropical rainforest. The road was bumpy, but the anticipation of what awaited us made every bump worth it. At the end of the track, we reached a small car park. From there, a narrow path led through thick forest. The descent was steep and required sturdy footwear, but with each step we felt the ocean drawing nearer. The sounds of the forest were gradually drowned out by the crashing of waves, and eventually, the trees opened up to reveal the ocean.

Whites Beach lay before us – a secluded white-sand beach, framed by towering cliffs and lush greenery. The water shimmered in the clearest shades of blue and turquoise you could imagine. It felt like we had discovered a hidden paradise.

We spent the day lying in the warm sand, swimming in the crystal-clear water, and simply doing nothing. No plans, no pressure, just that one moment, fully savoured. There were only a few people on the beach. The waves were calm, the sun was high, and now and then you'd hear us laughing, when someone slipped in the water or nearly gave themselves sunburn from lying in the sand too long.

The walk back was steep and our legs a little tired, but the day had more than been worth it. Even though we hadn't brought much—just some towels, a bit of water, and snacks, the day still felt complete.

That evening, after returning from Whites Beach, we met another special person at the hostel: Amira. She was German too, but with her darker complexion, brown eyes and hair, she looked more Mediterranean. We were surprised when she spoke to us in German. Amira was only 19, but the way she carried herself was so mature that we instantly got along. From that moment on, we spent nearly every day together.

The next morning, we decided to start the day with a walk to Cape Byron Lighthouse—the most famous lookout point in Byron Bay. With takeaway coffees from the hostel in hand, we set off early. The walk is about 3.7 kilometres (one way) and leads through an impressive mix of rainforest, open coastal scenery and steep cliffs. At a normal pace and with multiple photo stops—which are unavoidable, because everything is just so beautiful—you should plan around 1.5 to 3 hours in total. The higher you go, the more the view opens up.

On the left, the endless ocean. On the right, green hills dotted with small houses and palm trees. And in front of you: the lighthouse, perched on the cliff like something from a movie set. Once at the top, you're standing at the easternmost point of mainland Australia. And it really does feel a bit like standing at the edge of the world. You get a breathtaking view over Main Beach, Wategos Beach and, my absolute favourite—Tallow Beach.

If you don't fancy the walk, you can also drive up. However, parking is very limited and it's not cheap, 10 dollars per hour. The view is free only for those willing to make the trek on foot, and that's exactly why it was the perfect little morning walk for us. Though, honestly, calling it "little" is quite the understatement. It was a proper workout, the kind that leaves your legs burning and your breath short. But it was worth every step.

In Byron Bay, there wasn't really a single day where we didn't do something. Every day was filled with little adventures, spontaneous ideas, and moments that felt like scenes from a film.

One of those days took us to Tallow Beach — a stunning, expansive stretch of coastline located right behind the Cape Byron Lighthouse. The beach is less touristy than Main Beach, but all the more spectacular: crystal-clear water in every shade of turquoise, white, and deep blue. The shoreline is shallow, allowing you to wade in gradually, perfect for slowly easing into the waves.

For Marzio and Nici, it was their very first time on a surfboard. Nati and I had been surfing a few times before, but this was the first time the four of us were out in the water together, and that made it special. We helped the boys paddle out, gave them a few tips, and laughed ourselves silly when one of them immediately flipped backwards off the board on their first go.

Tallow Beach is ideal for beginners, as long as you stick to the rules. Depending on the section, the waves at Tallow Beach can be either gentle and long-rolling — perfect for softboards, or a bit stronger further out, ideal for more advanced surfers. But you really have to be careful there: the current can be tricky, and it's often underestimated how quickly you can get swept away.

On one particular day, I would learn that lesson the hard way, and someone literally saved my life. But that story will come later.

On another day, the four of us drove out to Killen Falls, about 30 kilometres southwest of Byron Bay. The drive took around 25 minutes, winding past green hills, narrow roads, and a real taste of the Aussie hinterland. We parked above a small nature reserve and made our way down a short but steep bush track. The closer we got, the louder the sound of rushing water became, and once we reached the bottom, we stood in front of a near-perfectly round waterhole and a wide, thundering waterfall cascading down a lush, green rock wall. The highlight? You could actually walk behind the waterfall. And of course, that's exactly what we did — soaking wet, laughing, and keeping the camera safe somewhere in the distance.

Later that evening, back in Byron Bay, we grabbed some fish and chips from a small but popular takeaway right by Main Beach. With our dinner in hand, we sat down on the grassy patch by the sea.

The sun was slowly setting, painting the sky in shades of orange and pink, and the sound of the ocean grew softer. We sat there with salty skin, messy hair and full bellies, simply content. Amid all the adventures, beach days and endless conversations, we also wanted to stay physically active.

Sure, surfing was already a workout in itself. It keeps you fit, makes you strong, lifts your mood and definitely helps you look young and healthy.

But still, we didn't just want to drift along, we wanted to look after ourselves a little, too. So we started doing small workouts together at the hostel. On the grass, in a quiet corner somewhere, or even right in our room if need be.

Unfortunately, backpacker hostels don't just attract friendly and honest people. One day, after doing my laundry, I hung my favourite pair of joggers on the line to dry, nothing unusual. But when I came back later, they were gone. Vanished without a trace. At first, I thought maybe someone had taken them by mistake, or picked them up by accident. But they never turned up. And at some point, it became clear: someone had stolen them. They were just a simple pair of grey Nike trackies. Nothing fancy or expensive. But to me, they had a certain value, especially when you're travelling, where you only have a few belongings with you and every piece of clothing suddenly plays its own little role in your daily life. I was genuinely disappointed. Not just because they were gone, but because it was one of those moments where you're reminded that travelling isn't always carefree and light.

And then there were evenings that made everything okay again. One of them was our jogging evening, just Nati and me.

It was late afternoon, and we felt like moving our bodies, so we laced up our runners and set off. We had no idea that this run would end in a small natural wonder. The sky felt heavy, dark, almost threatening. You could sense in the air that the rain wasn't far off. The setting sun broke through a gap in the thick blanket of clouds and cast the entire sky into a spectacle of colours we'd never forget. Above us, the clouds exploded in glowing pink, deep red, warm orange and dark violet – like a painting, like a portrait you'd hang in a gallery. The colours looked like they'd been squeezed from pomegranate seeds, wild and rich, as if someone had splashed watercolours across the sky.

One day, we felt like going on a little trip, a short escape from Byron, into the green, to explore something new. As on most days, we set off with Marzio and Nici, and this time we had something rather special on the agenda: the jungle camp. Yes, the

»*I'm a Celebrity – Get Me Out of Here!*«.

that millions of people in Germany watch every year is actually filmed in Australia, and not all that far from Byron Bay. The filming location lies deep in the greenery, in the area around Dungay Creek near Murwillumbah in New South Wales. Of course, the site itself is strictly off-limits, but just the idea of getting close to the place where so many celebrity dramas had unfolded was enough to spark our curiosity. Typical Germans, really – curious, detail-loving, and always up for a little adventure.

So off we went. Nici and Marzio in their 4WD, us in our trusty Goldi. And what a ride it was: the road quickly turned into a bumpy track. It went up and down hills, through deep potholes, muddy bends and narrow lanes. We were crying with laughter trying not to get stuck, cheering for every metre we managed to conquer. Eventually, it became clear that we weren't far from the actual camp. But it definitely didn't feel like a warm welcome. The locals seemed to know exactly why we were there, and they didn't seem to find it nearly as entertaining as we did. We had just parked the car, trying to get our bearings and maybe catch a glimpse of the surroundings, when suddenly a rather irate local appeared.

He jumped out and started shouting, accusing us of trespassing on private property and threatening to call the police. We stayed calm and polite, explained that we'd only just arrived, meant no harm, and would turn around immediately. But he wasn't having it. And right in that moment – just when the tension had hit peak level – his goat jumped onto our car bonnet. We just stared, wide-eyed, trying not to burst out laughing. I couldn't help myself and said:

»*You're more than welcome to call the police, and I'll make sure to mention that your goat just damaged our car*«.

That seemed to throw him off for a second. Maybe he realised not everything needed to escalate, especially not when your own goat is at the centre of it all.

We apologised again, explained we genuinely didn't know the area was restricted, and said we were already on our way out. Then we climbed back into the car and drove off, with a few fresh scratches, but one hell of a story to take home.

We didn't end up seeing the jungle camp, but that spontaneous little road trip through the Aussie "jungle" was absolutely worth it.

In between all the day trips, beach sessions and sunsets, we also discovered a new passion in Byron Bay: longboarding. Neither of us had really tried it before, but in this town, where everyone seemed to glide barefoot on some kind of board, we simply had to give it a go. The streets in Byron are made for it – long, palm-lined, with gentle slopes, smooth asphalt and that laid-back vibe that makes you want to just roll along and enjoy the ride.

We browsed through a few cool surf shops, not just packed with surfboards, but also stocked with longboards in every shape and colour imaginable.

In the end, I didn't even need to buy one. A friendly guy from the hostel – an English bloke, offered to lend me his. His name was Adam. Adam was one of those people who just belonged in a place like Byron, as if he'd been washed up by the ocean and never left. Tanned, well-built, sun-bleached mid-length hair, warm brown-golden eyes, tattoos that covered most of his body, and a smile that instantly lifted the mood. He was attentive, funny, more thoughtful than you might expect at first glance, and somehow… special.

We met him one warm evening while we were playing cards outside with Marzio and Nici. He joined in like it was the most natural thing in the world, introduced himself with a grin, and stayed. From that night on, he became part of our little circle.

Over the next few days, we kept hanging out. Sometimes casually at the beach, sometimes deep in conversation about life, sometimes cruising through town on longboards under the golden light of the setting sun. It would be a lie to say he didn't stir something in me, in his own quiet way.

Back then, I think I fell for him a little. Or maybe it was more a fascination – with the way he lived, the freedom he radiated, that effortless way of just being. He sparked something in me that I still carry with me. But whatever it was between us, it was part of the journey. Part of my path.

Sometimes, we meet people not to hold on to them, but just to open our hearts a little wider. Not because they're meant to stay, but because they show us just how much space there really is.

One of those days, Nati, Amira, Marzio, Nici and I decided to go surfing together again. Our destination was once more Tallow Beach, which kept drawing us in with its vastness, clear water, and those perfect waves. The way to get there was a bit of a hassle, you had to walk a fair bit, and parking was limited. During the COVID period, access had even been partly closed off, leaving the beach almost deserted at times. Now it was open again, but if you came by car, you'd need a bit of luck to score a spot. We were lucky, and more than ready for some waves. That day, however, we had no idea what was coming. Amira, Nati and I walked into the water together, surfboards in hand, ready to dive into the swell. Amira was in the middle, Nati on her right, me on the left. The water was shallow and calm, and the entry stretched out gently into the ocean as it always did.

Then, suddenly, I felt something slimy under my foot — soft, slippery, strange. I flinched, instinctively turned to the side, but couldn't see anything. I didn't think much of it, since it didn't hurt, but then, it happened.

Amira screamed. A piercing, panicked scream that sent a jolt through all of us. When I turned to her, I saw her flinch, then collapse into herself — and suddenly, there was blood in the water. Without hesitation, we all flung ourselves onto our boards, not just to stay close to her, but because none of us knew what was under us.

Was it a bite? A sting? Some kind of creature still nearby? Amira clenched her teeth, trembling, her eyes wide and full of pain. Blood streamed down her foot and along her leg, and there was a lot of it. We yelled at her to lift her legs out of the water, not to let them hang — instinctively, because in Australia, the thought of sharks is never too far away.

We weren't far out, but in a moment like that, the beach always feels miles away. Together, we paddled, a few metres that felt like forever, driven by adrenaline and fear. Amira clung to her board, eyes tightly shut, barely able to speak. When we finally reached the shore, she practically collapsed off her board and dropped to her knees. Her foot was torn open along the side — a deep, clean cut, bleeding heavily. Blood was everywhere. It looked like something out of a movie, except this time it was real.

I sprinted to our bags, grabbed a towel, anything I could find, and we wrapped it around her foot, trying to stop the bleeding. And then, as if someone had perfectly timed it for dramatic effect, Adam came running. The English guy from the hostel. Tanned, serious, focused. I had to blink. For a brief moment, it felt like a scene from Baywatch — only without the slow-motion, the rescue float, or Pamela Anderson. Instead, Adam, our own emergency Adonis, came charging across the hot sand. He wasn't a lifeguard, not a paramedic, but he sure looked the part.

He'd seen everything from the beach and didn't hesitate for a second. Marzio also came running and took over when we realised Amira couldn't walk. He lifted her onto his back and carried her across the sand towards the car park. Meanwhile, we'd already called an ambulance.

Later, we found out what had happened: Amira had been stung by a stingray. Most likely, I'd stepped on it with my foot, it got startled and shot off, straight in her direction. The wound came from a direct strike with the venomous barb on its tail. It was a shock. But at the same time, we were beyond grateful that it was just a stingray, and not something worse.

Later that day, Amira was taken to hospital by ambulance. We stayed behind at the roadside for a while – soaked, barefoot, hearts pounding, watching the ambulance drive off. It was that strange mix of exhaustion, worry, and relief that help had come so quickly.

At the hospital, the cut on her foot was thoroughly cleaned, stitched, and heavily bandaged. The doctors confirmed it had been a stingray – a rare but not unheard-of encounter in Australian waters.

The injury was deep and painful, but luckily, not life-threatening. As a precaution, Amira had to stay overnight for observation, in case of infection or an allergic reaction to the venom.

The next morning, we picked her up again. She was already waiting in a wheelchair at the exit, foot heavily bandaged – but with a big grin on her face.

*»In a few days, I'll be back on the board«,*
she said with a wink. We all burst out laughing. Her

humour, her strength – that was so Amira. She wasn't going to let a stingray take her down.

The weeks we spent in Byron Bay flew by. By now, we'd been there for over two months, and each day felt like a little adventure. We lived in the moment, soaking up the sun, the ocean and the joy of being together. The sunrise surfs at Wategos Beach were especially unforgettable. This beach, nestled in a protected bay, offered long, gentle waves – perfect for longboards and chilled-out sessions. The vibe was peaceful, almost meditative, and the water shimmered in the most stunning shades of blue. Parking was limited and often packed, but that didn't stop us from returning again and again.

Another highlight was The Pass. This stretch of beach wasn't just known for its powerful waves, but also for its breathtaking scenery.

It lay directly below Cape Byron Lighthouse, and from up there, you could watch the surfers glide across the waves as if they were floating. There was something almost hypnotic about it, watching them again and again, never getting tired of it. The sound of the crashing waves, the calls of the seagulls and the warm breeze coming in from the ocean made this one of the most magical places in Byron Bay.

Our days were filled with shared activities, little rituals and spontaneous ideas.

We threw beach parties at Main Beach, dancing in the sand, strumming guitars and laughing until late into the night.

Back at the hostel, we'd organise laid-back Monopoly nights, drinking games or simply sit on the terrace chatting for hours. We explored the area on foot, by car, or sometimes without any plan at all, just letting the day take us where it wanted. Every day felt different, but never meaningless.

One especially beautiful day was our trip to Broken Head. That morning, we packed our surfboards and set off with Nici, Marzio, Nati and Adam. The drive there was already part of the experience – windows down, music playing in the background, everyone in a good mood. Broken Head was less crowded than other beaches, untouched, with small rocky sections lapped by turquoise water. We surfed, lay in the sand for hours, listened to music and snacked on the typical Aussie crackers that seem to belong in every beach bag. It was one of those days when everything felt light and just right, like a holiday right in the middle of everyday life.

One moment with Adam has especially stayed with me. We were lying a little apart from the group in the warm sand, gazing out at the ocean, talking about life. No shallow small talk, but conversations with depth – about goals, dreams, fears, the things that truly move us.

I love those kinds of conversations. They give me a sense of connection, when I can truly open up to someone without having to pretend. I like people with whom you can simply be yourself. Where it's not about being funny, strong or perfect all the time, but just honest.

That day with Adam, I had exactly that feeling, and it did me a world of good.

Another little ritual of ours was the daily visit to the gelato shop in Byron Bay. Nati loved ice cream more than anything, and her excitement rubbed off on all of us. The ice cream shop offered a wide variety of delicious flavours and quickly became a regular part of our daily routine.

Our hostel also had turned into a home for an international community. People from Argentina, Spain, France, Germany and many other countries came together, and we became one big family – laughing, learning, and enjoying life to the fullest.

But there were also those quiet days – days when we just stayed at the hostel, hung out by the pool, or swayed in a hammock under a palm tree. Just switching off, resting, breathing. The sun on our skin, the soft rustling of the leaves above us, sometimes that's all it took for the moment to feel perfect.

On one of those relaxing days, we went snorkelling at White's Beach with Marzio and Nici. Although the water there was calm and clear and there was no reef nearby, we were lucky enough to spot a stingray. The water shimmered in a light turquoise, almost white – like a painting. It wasn't a place full of colourful fish or coral, but beautiful in its own unique way.

Nati and I also took some time just for ourselves. One day, we were alone at Tallow Beach, walking barefoot along the shoreline and collecting shells. Marzio and Nici were happy to sleep in and enjoy the peace and quiet, while we had the ocean and the silence all to ourselves.

In the evenings, things would often get lively again: There were barbecues on the hostel rooftop – with music, fairy lights, and the scent of grilled veggies, meat and toasted bread in the air. We sat in big circles, laughed, told stories, and everything just felt so light. There were countless game nights where we laughed until we cried. It felt like we weren't all just randomly staying at the same hostel, but as if someone had deliberately brought us together.

During our final days in Byron Bay, it slowly dawned on us that our chapter here was coming to an end.

The borders were open again, our visa clock was ticking, and we knew it was time to move on. But before leaving the coast behind, we wanted to soak up Byron one last time.

One of our farewell trips took us to Nimbin – a small town about an hour away, famous for its vibrant hippie culture, colourful murals, quirky shops and a vibe all of its own. It felt like stepping back in time as we strolled down the tiny main street. While wandering through a souvenir shop, Nici discovered what was possibly the ugliest pair of shoes Australia has ever produced – FISH sandals. Yep, actual shoes that looked like fish: the open fish mouth at the front for your toes, and a tail fin at the heel. They looked so ridiculous that we laughed until we cried. I can't even remember if he ended up buying them, but the image of Nici wearing those things will stay with me forever.

Of course, we also quickly noticed what Nimbin is known for – weed. It wasn't exactly a secret that plenty of backpackers came here for that very reason, and you could definitely feel like you'd entered another world. Everywhere you looked there were bright colours, incense, reggae music, peace signs and dazed-looking folks in tie-dye shirts. It was like stepping into a living flashback of the 70s. It felt like we'd left modern Australia behind for a while and entered a quirky little hippie world with its own rules.

Still, the place had charm – a bit odd, but also fascinating. Definitely a stop you won't forget in a hurry.

Back in Byron, we got lucky one evening and caught one of the town's most popular street performers live: Felipe Baldomir – the good-looking surfer with a soft voice and deep, soulful eyes. Back then, he was playing together with Tay Oskee, another talented musician, and just like so often in Byron, a crowd had gathered, dancing barefoot on the pavement, laughing, clapping, and simply letting go. Music is just part of the air in Byron Bay, it's everywhere.

Another day, Nati and I set off once again for the lighthouse – or at least, that was the plan. We had completely ignored the weather, full of anticipation for one last walk. But about halfway there, it started to rain. Not just a drizzle. It poured down in buckets. Within minutes we were soaked, our clothes stuck to our skin, and we couldn't stop laughing. We ran through the streets, dripping wet and happy.

Back at the hostel, we literally had to pour the water out of our shoes – no joke, it was flowing out in streams. It was one of those little moments that burn themselves into your heart, simply because it was so real. No plan, no filter, nothing staged. Just the two of us, soaking wet, laughing, right in the middle of the downpour while all of Byron Bay disappeared beneath grey clouds.

And yet, not a single thought of wanting to escape or feeling annoyed. Just that childlike joy of feeling utterly alive.

Since we had to literally leave the lighthouse standing in the rain that day, we decided on the spot to just try again. The next day: new day, new luck. This time, the weather was on our side, and we arranged to meet a few others from the hostel for a little sunset picnic up at the lighthouse. An evening at the lighthouse with sushi, sunset, and good company.

We sat on the small grassy patch, watching the surfers ride the final waves of the day, while a few dolphins glided quietly through the bay. The sun painted the ocean in golden hues. Everything was calm. Just the sound of the ocean, our laughter, and this feeling of gratitude.

Time had flown by far too quickly. Almost four months we'd spent here already. Months full of stories, sunsets, laughter, new friends, and unforgettable days.

We knew the end was near, so we decided to make the most of our final days: one more surf, one last visit to our favourite places. And of course: a little farewell party at the hostel, where we could say goodbye to everyone once more. It wasn't easy. Byron Bay had become a home. But our journey wasn't over yet.

On one of our last days in Byron Bay, we wanted to go all in again. One final surf at Tallow Beach, one last ride on the waves, or so we thought.

It was late morning, the sun already pleasantly high, but the beach was unusually empty. Perhaps a sign we should have taken more seriously. Nati, Amira and I – our usual little trio, grabbed our boards and headed out into the water. The conditions seemed alright at first, the waves a little stronger maybe, but nothing out of the ordinary.

But the longer we stayed in the water, the clearer it became: the current was extreme. Without realising it, it had slowly carried us further and further out, away from the safety of the beach, towards the cliffs on the left-hand side – the ones with the lighthouse perched above. Beneath us, the rocks had turned sharp, the water was deep, and the ocean floor had long disappeared.

We tried to fight it, paddled hard, desperately trying to make our way back to shore, but we weren't moving an inch. Our arms were burning, our strength fading, and panic began to rise. Waves slammed us against the rocky shoreline. We were out of options. All around us was just water and the threatening sound of the crashing sea. For a brief moment, we even considered paddling all the way around the cliffs – a desperate idea, as the distance was far too great.

Then, out of nowhere, two surfers rushed into the water from the beach. They must have realised we were in serious trouble, perhaps they had seen our frantic movements and the sheer panic on our faces.

Nati and Amira were a bit closer to shore than I was; they were already fighting hard against the current. I, on the other hand, was further out, driven deeper into the open ocean – caught between rocks, waves, and that dark, endless unknown beneath me.

The two surfers headed straight for Nati and Amira, calling something out to them, trying to calm them down, giving them instructions. Together, they worked to get them back to shore – metre by metre, wave by wave. It was a massive effort, because even with their experience, it was hard to fight the water. The current wasn't letting anyone go easily.

I watched them drifting away, saw Nati and Amira slowly getting closer to the shore. And at the same time, I felt how far away I still was.

Completely alone in this vast, unpredictable ocean. And then, Adam appeared. Out of nowhere, of course. Paddling towards me on his surfboard, calm, determined, and focused.

*»Anne,, deep breaths. We've got this«,* he said.

No room for drama, just solutions. He explained that we first needed to paddle further out, away from the dangerous breaking current, and then try to ride a big wave back in towards shore. I was scared. More than ever before. The water beneath me was black and endlessly deep. I had never been this far out, never felt this vulnerable.

Then came the wave. One of those long, powerful waves that either carries you… or takes you under. I felt it building beneath me, got ready, and stood up – even though Adam had told me to try it lying down, since I barely had any strength left. I could hardly stay upright, lost my balance, and fell. But: I was much closer to the shore. Adam was right there again, paddling next to me, calling out over and over that I couldn't give up.

*»You have to paddle. Just keep paddling.«*

And that's what I did. Every metre felt like a kilometre. I had no energy left, only fear and adrenaline.

Eventually – finally, we reached the shore. I let go of my board, collapsed onto the sand, gasping for air. My legs were shaking, my heart was racing. I fell into Adam's arms. I couldn't stop crying – out of relief, out of gratitude. In that moment, he had saved my life.

Shortly after, Nati and Amira arrived too, together with the other surfers. They were exhausted, but safe. I looked at Nati's face and saw that she knew how close it had been. And when we were all hugging each other again, I could hardly believe what had just happened.

Later, when things had calmed down a bit, I told the others that I was almost certain I'd seen a shark in one of the waves. I remembered the shape – maybe a hammerhead, or maybe just a shadow. But in that moment, in such an extreme situation, it felt real. And even if it wasn't: the fear, the uncertainty, the feeling of being completely powerless, all of it was tangible. It was a moment that changed all of us. Not just because of the fear, but because of what it showed us: how precious life is, and how quickly everything can flip, from a carefree surf day to a fight to make it back to land. A fight we got through together.

If you now think that after that day – after all the fear, the panic, the tears, and the feeling that I might've come a little too close to death – I never touched a surfboard again, you'd be wrong.

The next morning, I went back into the water. Maybe it was defiance, maybe it was healing. Or maybe it was simply that special kind of energy Byron Bay gave me – this feeling that everything had meaning, even the difficult moments.

That evening, we had our farewell party at the hostel. We

all knew that the next day, our journey would continue. There was no rush, just a little time left to close a chapter. A chapter that had become so much more than just a place. It was the heart of our trip. Without a doubt, the best time we'd had in all of Australia.

Byron Bay was our number one. It felt like a temporary home. A home for the soul. Saying goodbye was hard. Tears were shed. Hugs lingered a little longer than usual. Glances spoke louder than words. We had become a family, thrown together from all corners of the world, connected by a shared time we would never forget.

And for me, it was more than just a farewell. It was the moment when everything inside me began to realign.

It was in Byron Bay that I made my decision: I wouldn't return to Germany. I wouldn't just stay for a year. I wanted to stay – for good. Australia was the first place that had ever truly felt like home. Not because it was perfect, but because I had finally arrived in myself. I don't really know how to explain it, but it felt like the wind carried something different here. As if it whispered:

*»This is where you're meant to be.«*.

And that's exactly why this book is called 'When the Wind Changed'. Because in Byron Bay, it wasn't just the direction of the wind that changed – my whole life did.

# CHAPTER EIGHTEEN
## HEADING SOUTH

That afternoon, Nati and I left Byron Bay – our home for the past few months, with hearts full of memories we'd carry with us forever.

Our first stop was Coffs Harbour, about 230 kilometres further south. The drive along the coast took roughly two and a half hours and led us through picturesque scenery, past small towns and endless stretches of beach. Coffs Harbour welcomed us with its relaxed vibe and the fresh ocean breeze. One of the most striking features was the historic jetty, a wooden pier over 100 years old that stretches far out into the sea. Originally built in the late 19th century to export timber, it's now a popular spot for sunset lovers, anglers and casual walkers. From the jetty, you get a breathtaking view of the Pacific Ocean and the surrounding coastline.

After a relaxing walk along the jetty and a brief visit to the marina, where we watched the boats bobbing in the water and soaked in the salty air, we wound down the evening peacefully. It was the perfect start to our new adventure – a gentle transition from the familiarity of Byron Bay to the unknown roads that lay ahead.

But that evening, as we cooked dinner at a small free campsite nearby and watched the sun slowly set, we felt it for the first time – the absence of our friends. It was the first time in a long while that it was just the two of us again. No shared laughter with Marzio, no quirky jokes from Nici, no chaotic dinners where all four of us cooked together. We simply missed our little travel crew. Now it was just the two of us, sitting with our plates on our laps, feeling how different everything felt without the others around.

Mentally, we were still back at the hostel in Byron Bay, imagining them sitting together, laughing, maybe even playing Monopoly, and we missed them. We thought about them, our little hostel family.

But at the same time, we knew it was the right decision to move on. We hadn't come to Australia to stay in one place, but to experience the vastness of this country. New places, new stories, new encounters. That had always been our dream, and it was far from over.

The next morning, we woke up with a quiet certainty: we

were exactly where we were meant to be.

Still a bit tired, but full of anticipation, we hit the road – our destination: Sawtell Lookout. A small, barely known place, but perfect for one of those days when you simply want to breathe and feel alive. When we arrived, it took our breath away. In front of us stretched a sea of green, velvety hills, gently sloping down towards the ocean. We stood right at the top, on one of those hills, the grass lush and tall, and our view went straight out to the endless, deep-blue Pacific. Far below, the waves crashed against the rocky coast, while above us a few light clouds drifted by, carried by the wind like thoughts that didn't need to settle anywhere.

We spent the whole day there. Wandering barefoot through the grass, sitting down to silently gaze at the sea. We talked about everything – about our journey, about life, about dreams that were slowly turning into plans. It was one of those days where everything felt light, so light it seemed as if time had stretched a little, just for us.

Later, we climbed over the flat rocks, hopping from stone to stone. We found seashells so pretty and detailed it felt like the ocean had spat them out just for us, and the waves crashed rhythmically against the cliffs. It wasn't anything spectacular, not a famous spot on the map. But for us, it was exactly what we needed.

The next morning, we woke up with that familiar mix of excitement and a craving for adventure. The sun was already high in the sky as we hit the road—no fixed plan, but a clear intention to keep heading south. Our motto stayed the same: just go with the flow. Whatever looked good on the map became our next destination.

That's how we ended up at Hat Head National Park, a

hidden gem along the coast of New South Wales. The drive from Sawtell took about an hour and a half. We chose the Korogoro Walking Track, a roughly 3.2-kilometre loop that starts at the car park at the end of Ledge Street in Hat Head. The trail led us through dense coastal forest, past wildflowers, and offered breathtaking views of the ocean. While walking through the landscape, we encountered giant kangaroos for the very first time—those muscular animals you usually only see on TV. They stood just a few metres away, curiously watching us.

The track continued along the coast, past rugged cliffs where waves crashed dramatically against the rocks. We stopped for breaks, sat in the tall grass, and let our gaze wander across the endless blue of the ocean. It was one of those days where time felt like it had paused, just for us.

By late afternoon, we returned to the car park—exhausted, but filled to the brim with the impressions of the day. Hat Head National Park had deeply moved us with its raw beauty and unexpected wildlife encounters.

After our adventure in Hat Head National Park, where we'd explored the breathtaking coastline and come face to face with those massive, muscle-bound kangaroos, Nati and I continued our journey.

The next morning, we reached Port Macquarie – a charming coastal town known for its idyllic beaches and relaxed vibe. We spent the day collecting seashells and watching little silver fish darting through the crystal-clear water. I was so fascinated by them that I just had to film them with my iPhone. Unfortunately, I quickly learned that saltwater and iPhones aren't exactly the best of friends. Within no time, my phone was completely fried.

I could've cried, especially since we didn't want to waste our hard-earned farm savings on something so ridiculous. But, well, lesson learned, and just another story to add to the collection.

We immediately drove to the nearest town, hoping we might be able to save something. At the shop, we explained the situation and showed them the soaking-wet device, but the verdict came quickly and bluntly:

*»Sorry, that's gone. You'll need a new one«*

So I bit the bullet — or more like, bit into a brand new Apple, and did what had to be done.

Once the frustration had somewhat subsided, Nati and I set off for Black Head, hoping to at least end this chaotic day on a more peaceful note. The sun was already low when we arrived. The colours in the sky reflected on the water's surface, casting everything in warm hues of orange and pink. For a moment, the world seemed to slow down — peaceful, quiet, clear. We just sat there, staring out at the sea, without saying much. Sometimes you don't need big words, just a calm moment to make everything feel a bit lighter again.

The next day, our journey took us further to Wallis Lake —

a stunning body of water with turquoise tones and white sandy shores. We found a fallen tree stretching out over the lake, sat down on it, let our legs dangle, and soaked in the silence.

Later, we wandered along the lake's edge, discovered hidden trails and watched the gentle waves lapping against the shore.

In Tuncurry, the twin town of Forster — we prepared dinner: our famous fried potatoes with capsicum and that creamy chive dip we'd already loved so much back in the Outback. We sat on a bench by the water, next to the boats, and enjoyed the peaceful atmosphere. Our journey continued along the coast, past small villages, open fields, and once again, the calming sight of the ocean.

After a long day of driving with several stops and plenty of music in the car, we arrived in the late afternoon at Swansea Heads, a picturesque coastal town nestled between Lake Macquarie and the Pacific Ocean. The sun was already beginning to sink lower on the horizon as we explored the rocky shoreline. Among the crevices in the stone, we spotted tiny crabs that darted back into small tidal pools the moment we got too close.

The following day, we had a special destination on our list, one we'd been particularly looking forward to: Norah Head. The historic lighthouse towers proudly above the cliffs, almost as if it's watching over the land from afar. Ninety-six steps led us to the top, each one accompanied by a growing flutter of anticipation. Once at the summit, we were rewarded with a breathtaking panorama: expansive stretches of ocean glittering silver in the sun, white foam crests dancing over the reef, and a horizon that seemed to stretch out into infinity. We stayed up there for a while, leaning against the railing, gazing out silently – thoughtful, content, and completely in the moment.

A few days later, after continuing a little further south, we finally made our way to Palm Beach – the northernmost tip of Sydney. The atmosphere there was different: livelier, closer to the city, but still wild and untamed.

The path to Barrenjoey Lighthouse wound its way through green bushes and sandy hills until we reached the iconic lighthouse, proudly perched atop the headland. The view from up there was breathtaking. On one side, the vast, deep blue ocean stretched endlessly into the distance; on the other, the calm, sheltered bay of Pittwater lay still and peaceful. It felt as though we were standing between two worlds. These stops on our journey were more than just pins on a map. They were little chapters filled with encounters, discoveries, and in between, just regular days.

Each place brought with it a unique atmosphere, a different feeling, new conversations. It was never about seeing as much as possible, it was about truly experiencing each place.

Before heading into the final stretch towards Sydney, there were still two places on our list we absolutely didn't want to miss. Two places that had fascinated us for a long time, and that we couldn't skip before the big city swallowed us again.

The first was a natural highlight: the Blue Mountains. From Palm Beach, it took us around two and a half hours to reach the Blue Mountains National Park, which, in winter, is bathed in a light all of its own.

Although the Australian winter can't be compared to the icy frost we know from Germany, it was bloody cold up there in the mountains – even colder than we'd expected. At night, temperatures dropped to around 0°C. And us? Of course, we slept in the car again, on a campsite we had booked online beforehand. Despite two thick blankets and every piece of clothing layered on top of each other, we were half frozen the next morning. Looking back though, it was all absolutely worth it.

The Blue Mountains are simply breathtaking. The deep gorges, endless forests, and that mystical atmosphere created by the crisp mountain air and the ever-present veil of mist, it felt like another world entirely. We were especially moved by the famous Three Sisters – those three distinctive rock formations standing like ancient guardians over the valley. We stood there for ages, just gazing in silence. Afterwards, we continued on to the Katoomba Falls, where water crashes down the cliffs in multiple cascades. It was so beautiful, so peaceful, and at the same time so powerful. All the cold was forgotten, at least for a while.

We ended up staying two nights up there, just wanting to soak in everything, even if it meant shivering at night and needing hot tea in the morning to feel human again.

After that, we knew: we were ready for Sydney. But one last stop was still waiting for us, something truly special: the Figure Eight Pools.

These small, natural rock pools on the coast south of Sydney look like perfectly carved figure eights, and in good weather, they reflect the sky and sea in a surreal kind of beauty. What nobody told us, though: the path to get there is no casual stroll. It's a real hike. Not particularly steep, but long and exhausting. And then it rained. Of course it rained. Pouring rain. We should've known it wasn't ideal – but hey, you only live once. And we really wanted to see them.

So we trudged along the slippery trail, through the rain, the wet scrub, all the way down to the coast. Huge waves crashed against the rocks, the wind was wild, and the pools? Completely flooded. Nothing to be seen of the perfect circles. Just foaming surf, wild water, and a warning sign clearly stating how dangerous it was under these conditions. Still, it was special. Maybe even because it was so wild and rough.

We walked along the rocks for a while, watching the waves pound the coastline with full force. And then came the walk back. That part was… long, wet, and honestly exhausting. Our legs were aching, our clothes soaked and clinging to our skin – and still, we laughed. Because it was one of those moments that etched itself into our memories. A moment that reminded us: life doesn't have to be perfect to be unforgettable.

Our road trip was over. Truly over. It felt as if someone had closed the final page of a chapter too beautiful to end. Nati and I had spent nearly eleven months travelling across Australia together. We had worked, laughed, cried, argued, made up, and shared every single day. And now, we were standing at the beginning of a new chapter. The last road trip was done, the last shared destinations explored, and all that remained were two more weeks in Sydney before we'd say goodbye for good.

You might be wondering why I didn't fly home with Nati. But for me, it was clear: I wasn't ready. Something inside me told me that my time here wasn't over yet. I didn't know how, but I had to find a way to stay. I'd come up with a plan — somehow.

We spent our last two weeks together in Sydney at a hostel. This time it wasn't a private room; we shared it with two other girls, but that was fine. We were out all day anyway, exploring the city. The Harbour Bridge. The famous Opera House. Sydney was massive, overwhelming, loud — and truthfully, we were never really city people. It wasn't the most beautiful place of our journey, but the moments we shared there were still special.

One place that stole our hearts was Morgans Coffee Roasters. We crossed the entire Harbour Bridge on foot every single time just to grab our favourite coffee on the other side. Then we'd walk back with our cups in hand, watching the glistening water and the boats passing below. It all felt like something out of a movie.

On another day, we took the ferry to Manly Beach. There were surfers in the water again, and instantly it brought back memories of our time in Byron Bay. I felt this sudden urge to slip back into a wetsuit and run into the waves with a board. It was cold — still winter, but in my heart, it felt like midsummer.

On 17 June 2020, the time had come – the day I had to take my best friend Nati to the airport. Our shared journey, the one we had been looking forward to for so long, had come to an end.

Eleven months of adventures, challenges, growth, and unforgettable memories were now behind us. Eleven months during which we had been inseparable. We both cried our eyes out. Even on the train ride to the airport, we barely spoke. Our eyes said it all.

When Nati disappeared through security, it felt like a part of me was leaving with her. I knew she was also happy, to go home, to see Eric, her family – but that didn't make the goodbye any less painful.

Our friendship had changed during this trip. It had grown, beyond any boundary. It wasn't just friendship anymore, it was family. We'd experienced things together that no one else could ever fully understand.

Endless hours on the road, accompanied by the sound of music and our voices. Sunrises on deserted beaches, barefoot in the sand. Shared surf sessions in the cold water of Byron Bay. Fits of laughter, tears of fear during our dives, tears of joy when we saw the Great Barrier Reef for the first time or drove across Fraser Island with Eric. Or when we slept under the stars at Uluru, in the heart of the red continent.

All of it was a first. Our first big journey. In our favourite country. Together. And that bond – no distance, no country, no ocean, could ever break it.

I stood there at the airport, eyes full of tears, knowing: a new chapter was about to begin. Alone. But I was ready.

# CHAPTER NINETEEN

SOLO—TRIP

It felt strange to be sitting behind the wheel with no one beside me. For the first time in almost eleven months, the passenger seat was empty. No Nati laughing. No shared playlists, no joint commentary on the landscape or the next ridiculous roadside scene. Just me.

My heart felt heavy, the farewell had only been six days ago — and yet, I was already back on the road. Alone. But those who know me, know this: I'm good on my own. I can enjoy my own company, even love it. And that was exactly my task now: to find my way back to myself.

I had stayed in Sydney for a few more days, sorting things out, organising my stuff, getting the car ready for travel. Nati's scent still lingered in the air. Her voice still echoed in my thoughts, her tears at the airport hadn't quite dried and, neither had mine. And still, deep down, I knew: a new chapter was beginning. A different one. An important one.

*»Off I go.«*

My destination was uncertain, my plan vague — heading south, maybe Melbourne, maybe eventually Western Australia. The longing for open space, for the unknown, kept me going.

My first stop: the Sea Cliff Bridge. A spectacular road that curves like a ribbon above the wild ocean, clinging to the cliffside. On my right, the sea roared — endless, powerful, captivating. I imagined how breathtaking this place must look from above, seen through the lens of a drone, which I of course didn't own yet. Still, the moment felt special. I pulled over, let the wind sweep through me, and gazed out over the open water.

It was nearby that I spent my first night alone, on a free campsite, in the car, in the woods. Surrounded by other backpackers, a small pocket of safety. And you know what? I wasn't scared. Not in that moment. No uneasy feeling, no thought of danger. Just a sense of freedom.

I cooked dinner under eucalyptus trees, stared into the flames, listened to nature, and inside me, everything became quiet. Quiet, and somehow alive. It was the beginning of something new.

The next morning, I woke up with the urge to keep moving, not because I was in a rush, but because the road was calling. I had no fixed plan, just a general direction: to follow the coastline further south, to wherever I felt like going. I let myself drift, made a few short stops along the way, until late morning, when I arrived at a place I'd found on the map: Killalea Beach. Something about the name had drawn me in. And when I finally got out of the car, breathed in the fresh, salty air, and kicked off my shoes, I immediately knew this spontaneous detour had been worth it.

The sand beneath my feet was fine and warm, the sound of the waves steady and soothing — like the slow, peaceful breath of nature itself. I walked along the beach for a while, with no destination in mind, just following the rhythm of my steps. The sun warmed my skin, not too hot, not too cold, just right.

Then, all of a sudden, I noticed movement in the dunes. I stopped and couldn't believe my eyes: a small group of kangaroos, barely twenty metres away, dozing in the shade of the bushes. They seemed completely relaxed, almost as if they were just as surprised to see me as I was to see them. I sat down on the ground, quietly watched them, and tried to soak in every second of that moment.

Afterwards, as the sun began to set, I continued my drive. I had heard of a small, idyllic campsite not far away in Jervis Bay National Park, right on Bream Beach.

The recommendation had been spot on. The site was perched slightly above the water, nestled among trees, with a wide view over a quiet lake that turned golden in the evening light. It was peaceful, secluded, tranquil, like a hidden retreat far removed from the world.

Just a few steps down the hill, a narrow path led straight to the shore, where a simple wooden swing hung between two trees. That's where I sat in the mornings, coffee in hand, as the sun slowly rose over the water and bathed the surface in soft shades of orange. I was alone, but I didn't feel lonely. It was the kind of silence that doesn't feel empty, but soothing, like it clears your head.

All around the campsite, kangaroos moved about as if the place belonged to them – which, to be honest, it probably did. They were used to people, came up close, and even allowed a gentle touch if you stayed calm. There were no fences, no enclosures. They stayed because they wanted to, or hopped away if they felt like it.

In the evenings, as the light faded and I cooked dinner on my small stove outside, the possums would come out. Curious little creatures with big, dark eyes, cautiously inching closer. One of them even sat down next to my chair one night, staring at me as if trying to figure out what I was eating, as if I'd suddenly appeared in its living room.

I stayed there for about five or six days. I had time. Time to hike, to read, to write, to think, or sometimes, simply to do nothing at all.

These days didn't feel like a holiday, but more like a gentle pause. A moment in which you hear only yourself. No constant chatter, no distractions, no pressure to go and experience something. I didn't know yet where I wanted to go next. But for the first time, that didn't feel like a problem, it was simply part of the journey. In those days travelling solo, somewhere between secluded beaches, vast national parks and quiet campgrounds, I felt—perhaps for the first time in a long while, that I was truly arriving in myself.

It was the kind of calm that only comes when no one wants anything from you, when no one is talking to you, when there are no plans to be made and no deadlines waiting. Suddenly, there was space. Space for thoughts that hadn't had room before. Space to look back, undisturbed. And the more I thought about everything, the clearer it became how far I'd already come. Not because everything had gone perfectly, or because things had fallen into my lap by chance. It wasn't luck in the usual sense that had found me. It was the kind of luck you create for yourself—step by step, with every conscious choice you make, with every risk you take even though you've no idea how it'll turn out.

I'd left behind my old life, chosen uncertainty over stability, discomfort over convenience. And that's exactly why I was here now. In the middle of this breathtaking nature, on another continent, alone—and yet so deeply connected to what really mattered to me.

I thought back to my former life. To those years in the barracks. The rigid routine, the pressure to perform, that sense of being stuck. It was a life I'd lived without really questioning it. Because it was "safe". Because that's just what people do. But deep down, I had known for a long time that I wanted something else. Something freer. Something that would make me feel truly alive. I'd just never allowed that thought to grow, until one day, I simply couldn't ignore it anymore.

And now I was here. Far away from everything I used to know. And it didn't just feel right, it felt necessary. I suddenly understood why so many people dream of a different life, yet rarely find the courage to actually claim it.

Maybe out of fear. Maybe because they don't believe it could be possible for them too.

But that's the thing, it is possible. Not easy. Not convenient. But possible. It takes courage, endurance, and most of all, the decision to take that first step.

These days alone taught me how important it is to be enough for yourself. I truly enjoyed that time, in a way many people can't quite relate to. For some, the idea of travelling alone is unimaginable.

Even Nati once told me that she'd never have dared to do it without me, that she'd feel completely lost on her own. I could understand that. But for me, it was the opposite. I'm someone who's completely at peace with herself. I don't need much to be happy – no big audience, no constant company. I could travel the world on my own without ever feeling lonely. Maybe that's the biggest realisation of this time: that being able to be alone is a strength. That you don't have to fear your own thoughts if you're willing to listen to them, and that freedom often begins the moment you stop clinging to what you've already outgrown.

After leaving Jervis Bay behind, I made my way to Narooma – a small coastal town I hadn't really had on my radar before.

But the moment I arrived, I knew: this was exactly the right next stop. What impressed me most was the "Australia Rock", a massive boulder by the water with a naturally formed hole in the shape of the Australian continent. Okay, maybe with a bit of imagination. I balanced my phone on the nearest rock, set the self-timer, and climbed into this rocky "window". The photo honestly looked like something straight out of a travel magazine. A tripod would've made it easier. But hey – I'm Anne. Why take the simple route when you can do it the hard way?

Afterwards, I walked along the coast down to the jetty. I was looking forward to a peaceful view – but instead, I got hit by a full-on smell attack. It stank. Like old fish, harbour grime, decay – just pure "ugh".

All I could think was:
*»What the hell is that smell?«*

Then I saw the crowd of people all staring at the water, and that's when I spotted them: seals. Everywhere. Lazing about on the rocks, flopping around in the water, rolling, snoring, striking poses. Well, seals might be cute, but they stink to high heaven. Still, I couldn't look away. I mean, when do you ever get to see that many seals up close? And then it hit me:

*»If they're this chilled here, there's probably somewhere you can swim with them, right?«*

I did a bit of digging and yep, there were tours where you could snorkel with the seals. Totally my thing. It had been on my bucket list forever anyway. So I booked it.

The next morning, I was up early and ready to go. The water? Freezing. Like, really freezing. Not just cold-cold, but

*»What the hell am I doing here?«* freezing.

At least they gave us thick wetsuits – I swear, they were thicker than the mattress in my car. With a jump into what felt like minus ten degrees, the adventure began, and it was so worth it!

The seals were playful, curious, and not shy at all. They floated around us, spun in circles underwater, and sometimes came so close I couldn't help but laugh. Not once did I feel afraid – quite the opposite, I was completely mesmerised.

Sure, it's not everyone's cup of tea. If the phrase "wild animals in open water" gives you goosebumps, you might want to think twice. But if you're brave, if you're curious, you'll be rewarded. Because these kinds of moments – as crazy as they may seem, are the ones you'll never forget. That day with the smelly, charming seals of Narooma was definitely one of them.

After that exciting encounter, I was off again – next stop: the Pinnacles in Ben Boyd National Park. I'd only seen a few photos online beforehand, but what I found there absolutely blew me away.

The Pinnacles felt like something from another world. Towering, jagged rock formations rising into the sky – painted in vivid layers of colour, from deep rust-red to soft, almost pastel white. The striations ran through the rock like brushstrokes on a canvas. It looked like a mix of desert and Mars, only right on the Australian coastline.

I spent the whole day wandering around, stopping again and again to take in this surreal landscape. The path led past steep cliffs, through small patches of forest, across open clearings, always with a view of the ocean. It was quiet there, hardly anyone around. I could walk entirely at my own pace, think, observe, and feel.

In the afternoon, I reached a more secluded beach, not far from the Pinnacles. From the very first moment I stepped onto it, I knew this place was something special. Quiet, almost deserted, framed by gentle dunes, and the water — crystal-clear, shallow, almost like a natural pool where the light danced across the surface.

I walked slowly along the shore, my feet sinking into the damp sand, when I suddenly noticed movement in the water. I stopped, squinting into the sun, and then I saw them. Rays. Huge, grey rays, gliding through the water with such elegance and weightlessness that for a moment, I thought I was dreaming. As if someone had perfectly choreographed the scene.

Their bodies swayed gently with the current, their wings moving in slow, graceful waves, almost as if they were dancing. My heart started racing, and I instinctively reached for my GoPro.

Luckily, I had it with me this time. Because over the months, I had learned how quickly these special moments could appear. There had been plenty of days where I had left my camera gear in the car, thinking nothing exciting would happen anyway, and those were always the days when the most magical things occurred. The light would be perfect, nature would show off in the most stunning way, or something completely unexpected would happen, and there I was, unable to capture any of it. That lesson had burned itself into my memory. From then on, I took everything with me. Even if it was heavy, even if I thought I wouldn't need it. Because in Australia, you never knew what the day might bring. And this day was the perfect proof of that.

Carefully, I placed the camera in the water, hoping to get a few shots of this incredible moment. I moved as little as possible, not wanting to disturb them. But they didn't seem scared at all.

On the contrary, one of the rays swam directly towards the camera, as if curious about the strange object in the water. For a brief moment, it came so close to me that I could've touched it. I held my breath. I was completely in that moment — no thoughts, no outside world. Just the ocean, me, and these mesmerising creatures. I could hardly believe my luck. The footage I got was incredible, but even more powerful was the feeling itself. That honest, quiet awe. I grinned like a kid at Christmas – filled with excitement, joy, and a kind of gratitude that words simply can't capture. No filter, no music, no Instagram story could've ever conveyed what that moment truly felt like. Just me, the sea, and the stingrays.

After all those weeks travelling solo, it eventually dawned on me: I needed a new visa. My time was running out, and even though I wasn't ready to leave Australia just yet, I had to start figuring out what came next.

Since I'd stayed in the country during the Covid period, I was eligible to apply for a special Covid-19 visa – a temporary option for anyone who had been stranded or restricted by the pandemic. And yes, even though life felt somewhat more normal again, Covid was still very much a thing. The borders to Western Australia were still closed, I had just left Sydney, and huge parts of the country were still difficult to access.

I filled out the application online, without expecting much – and just two days later, I got the confirmation: another three months in Australia. I could've burst out laughing. Three months. Another three months for me, for this country, for new memories.

But... I was also nearly broke. The travel, the food, the petrol, the hostels – I was now paying for everything on my own. No shared expenses anymore, no splitting fuel costs, no joint grocery shopping. I was still getting by, but my bank account was clearly telling me something needed to change soon.

Right on cue, a friend messaged me on Instagram after seeing my story – Alexa. Maybe you remember her – one of the two girls we met at the waterfalls in Queensland at the very beginning of the trip. That was almost eight months ago.

»*Hey Anne, if you need a job, we're looking for people here!*«.

She was working in a small town called Orange and said I should just give her boss a call, maybe it would work out. I didn't think twice. Not only because the timing was perfect, but also because I knew I needed the money.

A few days earlier, I'd been on the phone with my family. My mum had asked me, sounding genuinely concerned:

»*How much money do you actually have left in your account, Anne? Should I be worried?*«

My answer:

*»Don't worry, Mum. I've still got ten dollars – all good«.*

I couldn't stop laughing. Back in the day, something like that would've completely stressed me out. But now? I was cool as a cucumber.

Australia had changed me. I'd become more relaxed (maybe a bit too relaxed). I just thought: it'll be fine. Something always works out. And maybe Orange was exactly where I was meant to be at that time.

The fact that Alexa randomly saw my story all those months later, that couldn't just be a coincidence.

# CHAPTER TWENTY
## ORANGE

After I got the job in Orange over the phone – not exactly my dream job, but just what I needed at that moment – I hit the road, heading from Batehaven towards Canberra.

The drive wasn't too far. Just under three hours lay ahead of me, winding through gentle hills and dry, wintry landscapes. I had no stress, no fixed schedule, just myself and the music playing in the car. My destination: Canberra, the capital of Australia.

Many people tend to forget that, since Sydney and Melbourne usually steal the spotlight. But Canberra is the political heart of the country – meticulously planned, architecturally strict, almost a little too orderly. And that was exactly what made it interesting to me in that moment. I wanted to see something new again before diving back into work life.

I spent a few days in the city, strolling through the wide, almost empty streets, sitting in little cafés, letting my thoughts drift. Of course, I also visited Parliament House, the heart of the Australian government. The architecture was impressive – modern and clean, somehow fitting for a capital city more defined by functionality than flair.

One place that moved me far more than I'd expected was the Australian War Memorial. It's not just a regular museum you stroll through collecting facts, it's a mix of exhibition, archive, and memorial that brings the human stories behind the history to life. I especially remember the long hallway lined with portraits of fallen soldiers – each one showing a name, dates, and sometimes a personal quote or letter. Many of them were barely older than me.

In one of the exhibition rooms, personal items showed what everyday life during the war looked like, torn diaries, letters to families, uniforms with bullet holes. These weren't just anonymous objects on display – they were real stories, given a voice.

It reminded me once again how fragile peace really is. How lucky we are to wake up in the morning without fear, without having to say goodbye, without the noise of bombs or the pressure to defend ourselves.

I wandered slowly through the halls, read almost every sign, paused in front of the photographs, and listened to audio recordings. At some point, I stood in front of the "Roll of Honour" – a long wall engraved with the names of the fallen. Visitors place poppies between the letters – a quiet, powerful gesture of remembrance. That visit didn't just leave me thoughtful. It reminded me how often we take things for granted.

Canberra wasn't an exciting place in the traditional sense, but that was exactly what I needed. I could breathe, slow down, and reflect on everything that had happened over the past few months.

I knew a completely new chapter was about to begin – early mornings, physical work, new people, new routines. I had no idea how long I'd stay or what exactly was waiting for me, but I went anyway.

After a few days in Canberra, I packed up the car again and made my way to Orange. The drive took about three hours. Not particularly long, but far enough to feel like I was entering a completely different world once again.

Orange is located inland in New South Wales, about 250 kilometres west of Sydney and not too far from the Blue Mountains. That alone says a lot about the climate – instead of sea breeze, beaches, and palm trees, I was now greeted by the crisp, cold air of the Australian highlands. It was winter, and you could feel it with every breath. The town itself is charming and rather small, surrounded by hills, vineyards, and wide open fields. It's not your typical backpacker spot, but more of a quiet area known for its regional farming, wine production, and a growing food scene. For me, it was mainly one thing: a stopover. A place where I could settle for a while to top up my travel funds.

Since it got seriously cold at night in winter, I knew that

sleeping in the car wasn't an option this time. So I'd already looked for a room beforehand.

In Australia, many people rent out rooms privately or share houses with others. I actually got "lucky" and found a listing online in Orange that sounded promising. The landlord seemed friendly and said he travelled a lot for work. He lived in a small house a bit outside the city centre, and I was allowed to set up in a room at the back of the house. At first, I was relieved – a warm shower, a bed, a kitchen. All the things you learn to appreciate after weeks in the car.

But after just a few days, little things started to bother me. Nothing obvious, nothing dramatic, just that vague feeling that something wasn't quite right. There was a certain look, odd comments, and at some point, I simply didn't feel safe anymore.

But before I go into that, let me take you into my new everyday life – my job in Orange.

Before I officially started my new job at 'ALS Geochemistry' in Orange, I was lucky enough to catch up with my friend Alexa – the one who had told me about this job opportunity in the first place. It felt strange and at the same time really nice to see her again after all those months. The last time we'd met was somewhere in Queensland, ages ago, and now here we were, face to face in a small inland town in New South Wales.

Alexa was now working in a hair salon, even though she had zero experience in that field beforehand. The salon owner had trained her up, and they got along so well that Alexa not only worked there, she was also living with her. Her place felt warm and welcoming, a proper contrast to the weird atmosphere I was living in at the time.

We spent the evening cooking together and catching up on everything. It felt so good to have someone around again who was on the same wavelength.

Over the next few days, I used the time to settle into Orange. I went to K-Mart to pick up some essentials for my new everyday life — a thick blanket for the cold nights, work clothes, and other bits and pieces.

Then came my first meeting with my new boss. She explained the procedures, my work hours, pay, and everything else I needed to know. We completed the paperwork, and I received my personal protective equipment, including steel-capped safety boots — a must in this industry.

'ALS Geochemistry' is a lab specialising in geochemical analysis of rock and soil samples. My main role was in sample preparation: crushing rock samples using specialised machines, carefully packaging them, and recording everything in detail. These samples were then analysed in the lab to determine their metal content — for example, gold or copper. It was physically demanding work, but I was grateful to have some structure again and the chance to rebuild my travel budget.

In the first few days after moving into the accommodation in Orange, a kind of everyday rhythm started to return. I was waiting to begin work, spent time running errands in town, and tried to settle in as best as I could.

But even though my days were busy, there was a strange tension hanging in the air, a feeling I couldn't quite put my finger on.

The man I was living with seemed friendly and reserved at first glance, around five to ten years older than me. He worked during the day and usually came home in the late afternoon. But as soon as he walked through the door, the first thing he did was grab a beer from the fridge. Five minutes later, the next one followed. Then the next. This went on all evening. I watched this ritual and felt my discomfort grow. I've never been a big drinker, maybe one or two glasses of wine a month. So I struggled to understand this kind of behaviour. To me, it felt sad, even suffocating. I had the impression that alcohol had become a permanent fixture in his life. While I stood by as a quiet housemate, I couldn't help but wonder whether loneliness was the real root of it all.

This situation strongly reminded me of a time I thought I had long left behind — those weeks with Nati in Queensland, during our stay at our favourite farm with Mark. Back then, we lived with his friend, a woman who also drank daily, lived alone with her dog Sunny, and whose days followed the same worn-out patterns.

Here in Orange, it was almost the same picture, only this time, I was alone. The longer I stayed there, the more intense my uneasy feeling became.

My flatmate kept suggesting I come sit with him on the couch, have a drink, and watch TV together. I politely declined, but I could feel him watching me – while I cooked, while I spoke, during completely ordinary moments. It wasn't overtly threatening, but it was strange. Too intrusive. Too present. At night, my discomfort became even more apparent. All my life, my mum had drilled one thing into me over and over again:

*»Anne,, always trust your gut«.*

Don't try to push through with your head, don't always rely on logic or reason – instead, feel it, sense it, notice what feels right. And if something feels wrong, then walk away. I had followed that advice my whole life, and it had always been the right call.

Even here, in this dark, silent night, it was my gut that helped me realise just in time: I need to get out. I slept with my door locked – thankfully, as it turned out. Because I often heard him. First his footsteps, then suddenly complete silence. No sound, no movement, just this heavy presence in front of my door. He would just stand there. For minutes. I saw the shadow of his feet through the gap beneath the door – motionless, silent. My heart started pounding. I could feel my pulse throbbing in my temples, my chest tightening. This wasn't just a vague sense of unease anymore, it was fear.

*»What was he doing there? Why was he standing there for so long? What could possibly be going through his mind?«*

I could only imagine the worst-case scenarios, not because I wanted to overreact, but because my gut was clearly telling me: You're not safe here.

Looking back now, I'm more convinced than ever of how important it is to listen to that inner voice. Especially as a woman, especially when you're travelling, especially when you're on your own. It's sad that it's necessary, but I'd rather act early than find myself in a situation with no way out.

The next morning, I woke up early. He had already left for work. As soon as I was sure the coast was clear, I grabbed my bag, set it down, and started packing up all of my things as quickly as I could. I had only unpacked a few days earlier, but over a year in Australia had left me with quite a lot of stuff. Way too much, actually. But I knew I had to get out – now. Every move I made was accompanied by the nervous tremble of a single thought:

*»What if he comes back early? What would I say? How would he react?«*

Even just the thought of being alone with him again was unbearable. I had no excuse prepared, no explanation, and no idea what he might do. Maybe he'd get angry. Maybe... I didn't even want to think about it. So I acted. Quickly. Decisively. With my heart pounding in my throat.

I left the house and drove straight to Alexa. When I told her everything, she was shocked, but also exactly the support I needed. Even though she didn't have a spare room herself, she listened, she understood, and I finally felt a little safer again.

That same day, I jumped online and started searching for a new place to stay, and I found one. A couple had just posted an ad saying they were looking for someone. I wrote to them immediately, explained my situation honestly, and asked if I could come by. Their reply came quickly:

*»Sure, you can come over anytime«.*

Just a few hours later, I stood in front of Dani and Paul's house. I didn't know them, but the moment they opened the door, I just knew: This is the right place.

Dani was a few years older than me, her partner Paul about the same age. From the very beginning, they welcomed me with such warmth and genuine kindness that it nearly brought me to tears. They listened, reassured me that I was safe now, and told me I could move in that very night. No stress about the rent, that could all be sorted later. First, I should settle in. First, I should breathe.

They showed me my new room. Small, but cosy. Quiet. Safe. I dropped my bags, took a deep breath, and I knew: now my time in Orange could really begin. No uneasy gut feeling. No fear of the night. No constant tension in my stomach. I had finally found a place where I could feel at ease – and maybe, once again, this was exactly what I needed. A fresh start.

The weeks flew by faster than I'd expected. I spent them going to work every day, layering myself in three jumpers and two jackets in the morning to fight the freezing temperatures.

We started at five in the morning. At that time, it was still pitch black and bitterly cold. It was a different side of Australia, one I hadn't known before. Sometimes my windscreen would be completely frozen in the mornings, and I actually had to buy myself an ice scraper – in Australia! And while I stood there, all bundled up, my fingers nearly numb, I thought: Nope. I'm not ready to go back to Germany. This weather, this frost, it felt far too much like everything I had wanted to leave behind.

Between shifts at work, there was still time for friendship and small adventures. I spent a lot of time with Alexa. We did things together, cooked, laughed, shared our thoughts. She had become a real support for me.

Then there were my colleagues, almost all of them Italian. I don't know why, but I've always had a knack for getting along especially well with Italians. Maybe it's their open, warm nature, or the shared love for good food. In any case, I quickly found myself right in the middle of it all. I especially clicked with one colleague, Gloria. We went out for pizza, ordered tiramisu, spent evenings at her place, and it almost felt like being in an Italian share house right in the middle of the Australian winter.

Every now and then, I went on little solo trips. One day I drove to Mount Canobolas, and it snowed. Yes, snow. In Australia. I never would've believed it if I hadn't seen it with my own eyes. Snowflakes on Australian soil. Another moment that showed me just how multifaceted and surprising this country could be.

I also got on brilliantly with Dani and Paul. We went to pubs together, shared lots of laughs, exchanged stories.

Orange, this little inland town, had slowly grown on me. It reminded me a bit of an Australian version of a countryside village. Quiet, grounded, friendly. Not spectacular, but that was exactly what I needed at this stage of my journey.

Then I heard there was actually a way to extend my visa again, another so-called COVID visa, designed for people who were still in the country during the pandemic. Another three months in Australia. I couldn't pass up that chance. So I applied and waited, hoping to stay just a little longer in this country that had started to feel so much like home.

That morning, I left Orange and headed towards Sydney, just to get away for a few days, enjoy the sun, and escape the cold. It was only meant to be a quick weekend trip, something I'd been planning for a while. My own little escape plan from the chill. Out of the frosty winter air, and into the sun, by the sea. I wanted to see palm trees again, walk barefoot in the sand, feel the salty breeze. Maybe even go for a surf. I'd already pictured it all in my head: breakfast at Bondi Beach, sun on my skin, surfboards under our arms.

What I didn't realise was that I'd receive one of the most important messages of my entire trip on that very drive. While I was still on the road, the email came through: my COVID visa had been approved. I could stay in Australia for another three months. The relief was massive.

Because even though this visa – officially called the "COVID Subclass 408" – gave a lot of travellers hope during that time, it was never a sure thing. Every application meant waiting, hoping, and holding your breath. I always had this nervous knot in my stomach every time I submitted another request for approval.

I wasn't ready to go back. Back – to where, really? Germany hadn't felt like home for a long time. And Australia… Australia had become so much more than just a travel destination. It had become a place that felt right. Free, alive, wide open. I knew I wasn't done with this chapter of my life. Not yet ready to end something that had only just started to feel like a whole new beginning.

The drive from Orange to Sydney was around 260 kilometres – about four hours.

I remember being so present in every moment of that journey, knowing I'd been granted more time. That the adventure wasn't over yet.

What made the trip even more special was a long-awaited reunion: I'd made plans to finally meet up with Gina. A friend I'd first connected with through Instagram, way back at the start of my journey with Nati. Over the course of a year, we had messaged regularly, exchanged photos, sent voice notes, and shared our experiences, but somehow never managed to meet in person. One of us was always somewhere on the other side of the country. But now I was nearby, and so was she.

Gina was travelling through Sydney with her long-time boyfriend Eddie, and we quickly made plans to meet. We booked the same hostel, cooked dinner together, and talked for hours as if we'd known each other forever.

The next morning, we went out for breakfast and then actually hit the surf — well, I did. Gina didn't quite dare to get in the water, but she stood on the beach with her camera, cheering me on.

There I was, with a surfboard in the waves of Bondi Beach, laughing, feeling free, another bucket list moment ticked off.

As if that wasn't already enough, that weekend brought another reunion that meant a lot to me: Amira.

Maybe you remember — Amira from Byron Bay. The one we used to surf with nearly every day. The one who was stung by a stingray and ended up in hospital with a deep wound.

After all those months since our farewell in Byron, we

suddenly stood face to face again. She was living in Sydney now too, had settled into a hostel, and was finding her own path in her own way.

Our reunion was emotional — that familiar look, the warm laughter, the feeling that no time had passed at all, even though so much had changed in between.

We walked along the beach together, barefoot in the sand, as the sun slowly sank behind the waves. In the evening, we sat with a glass of wine on a small terrace, sharing all the stories that had happened since Byron – beautiful, wild, sad, surprising. Amira was still the same cool, strong woman I had grown so fond of back then. And yet, she had grown and evolved, just like I had. It felt good to share a part of this Australian journey together again, as if a familiar circle was closing, but without feeling like anything was standing still.

This little detour to Sydney was exactly what I needed in that moment. A break from being alone, honest conversations, and a familiar face.

It reminded me of what this country truly meant to me, not just because of the places, but because of the people I met along the way, who made it so special.

After this beautiful weekend in Sydney, I returned to Orange for my final two weeks of work there. I already knew that something new had found its way into my thoughts. Something I had missed more than anything. Even though I had been content, it didn't feel like the end. Something was missing. I just didn't feel whole yet.

During those two weeks, there was still something I needed to sort out — something that had been dragging on for months: our lost rear number plate.

Nati and I had lost it somewhere during our travels. But since our car was registered in Western Australia, it made everything a lot more complicated. Especially because the borders were still closed due to COVID-19. So I couldn't just drive over to sort things out in person. Not that it would've been realistic anyway — the distance from Orange to Perth is over 3,500 kilometres. A journey that would take several days by car. Completely absurd, but even trying to deal with it over the phone was a nightmare. Communicating with the Department of Transport was a total disaster.

They asked me to remove and send in not just the rear, but also the front plate, which meant I wouldn't be able to use my car anymore. But I desperately needed it to get to work.

Luckily, I had Dani, my landlord in Orange, who turned out to be a massive help. Since she was Australian and knew her way around better, she even came with me to the police station to officially report the loss. Together, we waded through the chaos of paperwork, follow-up questions and endless waiting times.

In the meantime, I was pulled over by the police several times, not out of bad intent, but simply because the missing plate stood out. Each time, I explained the situation patiently. Still, the whole process dragged on for over two months. In the end, I had no other choice: I reported the front plate as lost too, just to be able to get new ones at all.

And finally, after a long wait, I actually received two new

licence plates sent to New South Wales.

The old front plate, which I had never actually lost – I kept as a personal keepsake. It was dented, scratched, and full of stories, which made it the perfect souvenir of a time I would never forget.

But as if losing the number plate hadn't been enough, something else happened that really pushed me to my limit: the drive shaft of my car broke. I was out driving when I suddenly realised I couldn't steer properly. I was still able to brake, but the car barely responded. I was on a highway – completely overwhelmed, exhausted, and in bad weather. I just about managed to pull over to the side and called my workmates to see if they could pick me up.

The car was towed away, and at the workshop, the diagnosis was clear: the drive shaft was completely broken. Don't ask me how that even happens, I have no idea. But yes, it was dangerous and could've ended badly. I was just grateful it hadn't. The car had to be repaired, and I was without transport for a week. Thankfully, my colleagues were lovely enough to pick me up every day and drive me home again. Even financially, the damage was manageable. The whole repair only cost me $300, which, considering the circumstances, was actually quite reasonable.

But now, my time in Orange was coming to an end. Two intense, cold, yet enriching months lay behind me. I had learned a lot, met new people, and despite everything, experienced a beautiful stopover.

On my last day at work, I said goodbye to my colleagues – a moment I had mentally prepared for, but which turned out to be harder than expected. Saying goodbye to my Italian friends in particular touched me deeply. With them, I'd shared many funny, vibrant, and warm moments that would stay with me. Their openness, humour, and zest for life had enriched my time in Orange in a very special way.

For our farewell, we cooked together one last time. It was a small, but meaningful evening. The kitchen was bustling, we laughed, chopped vegetables, sipped wine, and talked about everything and anything. Everyone knew this was our shared farewell, and maybe that's exactly what made it so special. I soaked up every second, already knowing how much I would treasure this memory later.

I had already said goodbye to Alexa the night before. That hadn't been easy either. With her cheerful, easy-going nature, she had helped me through many heavy thoughts. She had been more than just a colleague to me, she had made me feel seen and accepted.

Our goodbye was quiet, almost uneventful, but deep down I could feel how much I was going to miss her. I hugged her one last time and thanked her for everything she had given me during that time – her support, her smile, her presence.

The next day, it was finally time to say goodbye – not just to work, but also to Dani and Paul, who had hosted me over the past few weeks. Their house had become my little refuge, a temporary home.

As I packed my things, I realised just how safe and welcomed I had felt in their presence. I thanked them from the bottom of my heart – for their help, their hospitality, their patience with my chaos, and most of all, for the warmth they had given me during such a sensitive phase of my life.

Time had flown by faster than I wanted to admit. My visa was coming to an end, and I knew a decision was looming. Should I return to Germany, to a life I had left behind? Or should I stay and find out what else Australia had in store for me?

*»Where would I spend my last two months in Australia? Where did I want to end this once-in-a-lifetime chapter of my life – in a way that felt whole and right?«*

It wasn't a decision I had to ponder for long. The state borders were still largely closed, and my options were limited. But even if they had been open, my heart had already made the decision long ago. There was only one place. A place that had never really left my thoughts. A place that had shaped me like no other. A place that had changed my life and shown me who I truly was. I knew instantly: I wanted to return to Byron Bay. Back to where I had first truly felt free. Back to where everything inside me had felt light and right. Back to where my journey hadn't started, but had transformed – into something bigger, deeper. I had missed Byron Bay. More than I could ever put into words. And now, the time had finally come to return.

*This time on my own, but with a destination that already felt like home.*

# CHAPTER TWENTY ONE
## WHERE I LEFT MY HEART

I had two months left. Two months in Australia before my visa would expire, before my Down Under chapter would come to an end and I would return to Germany.

Even though this time was incredibly precious, the decision about where I wanted to spend it was surprisingly easy. There was no doubt. No alternatives. No other place that could come close to what my heart already knew: I wanted to go back to Byron Bay.

Because if there was one thing I had learned on this long, intense journey, it was to listen to my gut, and my gut wasn't leading me somewhere new, it was leading me back. Back to the place where it all began. Where my thoughts felt clearer, and every morning came with the deep sense that I was exactly where I was meant to be. Byron Bay wasn't just a town to me. It was a feeling. A memory. A longing. A way of life.

༄

The journey from Orange to Byron was long. Almost 900 kilometres lay ahead of me, about ten hours of driving through the heart of New South Wales, past endless fields, small towns, and gentle hills. But not a single one of those hours felt like too much. Not a single kilometre felt wrong. Because each and every one brought me closer to where I truly belonged.

It felt like a journey through my innermost self, shedding everything that no longer suited me and making space for whatever was yet to come. I knew things would be different this time. I wasn't the same person anymore. I had changed, grown, experienced so much, and that's exactly why it meant so much to me to return. I wanted to spend my final weeks in Australia in a place that felt like home.

Sure, I could have said goodbye to this country with a smile from elsewhere too, but everything I'd experienced here had been too special. Byron was the missing puzzle piece – the place where everything could feel light, free and complete once more. Just the way I had hoped.

The closer I got to the coast, the more I felt everything inside me begin to relax. The landscape changed, the light grew softer, the ocean came closer, and at the same time, that feeling of coming home set in. Maybe for the last time.

When I finally passed the town sign of Byron Bay, a wave of emotion swept over me. It was as if this place had never forgotten me. As though it was welcoming me back with open arms, with familiar colours, and the same magic as back then.

I parked my car by the beach, took a deep breath, and let the salty ocean air flow through my body. I was back. And this time – I knew, I would savour every moment even more consciously, because I now understood how precious it truly was. Everything inside me went still. My heart, my mind – everything. And yet, beneath all this happiness, there was a quiet note of loneliness.

Because even though I had returned to the place I had loved so deeply, the people who had made that time so special were no longer here.

Nati, with whom I had stumbled through every single day for months. Marzio, Nici, Amira, Adam – all the people I had shared perhaps the most meaningful chapter of my life with, they had moved on. I was back. Alone. I was the new one. The girl stepping into circles that had already formed. The one who still had to find out whether this place was still the same without all those memories.

Sometimes it's not just the places that make memories so precious, but especially the people you share them with — and I was afraid that, without those people, I'd see Byron through different eyes. That it would feel different.

But Byron Bay surprised me. Once again. Because there's something about this place that stays, even when everything around you changes.

It didn't take long for me to meet new people. People who invited me into their little adventures, who took time for me, who were genuine, open, and free. People I went surfing with, did yoga with, sat on the beach with and laughed into the night. Byron gifted me with new faces, new stories, yet it still preserved that familiar feeling.

⌒

For the first three days, I stayed in a different hostel. Not the YHA I'd loved so much. My old home was fully booked. No surprise — now that the COVID situation had improved, more and more backpackers were flocking back to Byron. The town was suddenly full of life. A big contrast to the quiet pandemic months I'd experienced there before.

At the new hostel, I didn't feel entirely at ease. It wasn't bad, but it just wasn't the place I remembered. Not my YHA. But I knew: it was only for a few days. And sure enough, after those days, a bed at the YHA became available. I didn't hesitate for a second and secured my spot for the rest of the time I had left in Australia.

This time, I couldn't afford a private room. Instead, I shared with two other girls. Both of them were incredibly lovely, we hit it off straight away, and everything just worked. Still, it felt strange, like I was stepping back into a life that no longer existed.

When I finally moved back into the YHA, everything felt somewhat off at first. Familiar, yet foreign. The same walls, the same scent of backpacker life, the familiar sound of squeaky doors, but something had changed. Or rather: everything had.

I was beyond happy to be back, no question about that. But none of the faces I passed in the hallways, the kitchen or by the pool were familiar. I didn't know a single person.

Everything was new. Everything had changed. It felt like someone had pressed the reset button. Same hostel, same town, but a completely different chapter.

The longer I walked through the corridors, the more a strange feeling crept over me. I passed by the doors of the rooms where my friends once stayed, the ones I had cooked with, laughed with, surfed with, lived with. And now, there was nothing left of that. Just closed doors with unfamiliar voices behind them, voices I had never heard before. In those moments, it stung — almost like a knife to the heart. Not because anyone meant harm, but because it hit me: that chapter was truly over.

I never thought it was possible to feel so alone in a place that once felt so familiar. Of course, you always meet new people, that's one of the beautiful things about travelling. But once you've found your people, the ones who make everything feel easy and right, it becomes harder to open up to new faces again. Harder to trust. Harder to start over. And yet, here I was, ready to give it another go. With a lump in my throat, but also a quiet sense of hope packed in my bag.

I gathered all my courage, walked into the communal kitchen, and made myself some lunch. Everything felt a bit distant, like the gentle beginning of something new.

And then, in that very moment, he walked up to me: a friendly face, a warm smile, a relaxed gaze. Nil.

He introduced himself, asked if I was new, how long I'd been here. I told him my little story — about my months in Byron Bay, my travels with Nati, my time in Orange, and how I'd just returned. For my final two months. And that I couldn't imagine a better place to end it.

Nil and I clicked instantly. He was one of those people who

just made you feel comfortable. No fuss, no superficial small talk. Simply likeable.

Already the next day, he invited me to go surfing with him and a few others. We grabbed our boards, headed to the beach together, surfed, laughed, and soaked up the sun. Later, some of the guys played guitar. It was one of those days when everything felt easy. Effortless. Full of life. And even though we sat there with sand between our toes, salty skin, music in the air – I want to clarify something: these weren't hippies, and I myself was never part of the hippie scene that's often associated with Byron Bay.

Not that I have anything against it, really – but it just wasn't my thing. I loved the beach life, the freedom, the ocean, surfing, longboarding – all those small yet big things that made life there so special. But I wasn't the type for incense sticks, endless barefoot walks, or conversations about planetary alignments. I was more the kind of person who enjoyed life by the sea with a smoothie in hand and sunscreen on her nose, and that's perfectly okay.

When we came back to the hostel that evening, we were immediately drawn into a conversation with a few new people. The vibe was relaxed, almost like a big shared flat night – everyone lounging around on sofas, drinks in hand, laughing, chatting.

Amidst this hustle and bustle, I met Giulia. A young woman with a gentle smile, an Italian accent, and a quiet, reserved manner. She seemed shy, almost a little inconspicuous, but there was something about her.

The longer we talked, the more her true personality began to shine through: full of life, wonderfully quirky, and delightfully chaotic. Really chaotic, but in the most charming, lovable way.

I had only just met her, and yet it felt like I had known her for ages. We were completely on the same wavelength, and I just knew: this friendship would last.

Over the following days, I spent an incredible amount of time with Giulia and Nil. We just clicked without needing many words – and then, out of the blue, someone else joined us: Michela. And, how could it be any other way – she was Italian too. We often laughed about how random that was. Two Italian girls, a guy with Arabic roots, and me. None of us had known each other before, no one had travelled together, and yet we had all found each other right there, at the YHA in Byron Bay. As if we'd been scattered puzzle pieces, suddenly falling into place to create a small picture. And it was a beautiful one. Our own little crew, in the middle of so many unfamiliar faces.

We went on day trips together, had pizza nights, swam in the ocean, sat in the hostel courtyard in the evenings with a glass of wine in hand and shared our stories.

One of our favourite hangouts quickly became the restaurant where Giulia worked: Trattoria, probably the best Italian restaurant in all of Byron Bay. No surprise then that Michela and I practically became regulars there. Not just because we could visit Giulia more often, but also because the food was simply… a dream.

The pizza – my absolute favourite, was a work of art. Topped with fresh prosciutto, young baby spinach, fine truffle, and in the centre, a halved burrata sat like a crown. Burrata is that delicate Italian cheese with a firm mozzarella shell, hiding a luscious, creamy filling made from cream and cheese on the inside. As soon as you cut into the burrata, the soft centre slowly melts over the hot pizza and blends with the truffle flavours. It was the perfect combination!

And the best part: since Giulia worked there, Michela and I only had to pay half price. That made it taste even better, of course. So the Trattoria became our little regular spot. Our conversations, our laughter, our tiramisu at the end – all memories I'll cherish forever.

The four of us – Michela, Nil, Giulia and I, quickly became inseparable. Each day was different, but always full of those little moments that warm the heart. And many more wonderful people joined us along the way. Our little group, which had formed more or less by chance, grew day by day into something truly special.

Eventually, Opal joined us too – a kind-hearted, loving soul who was travelling around Byron with her equally lovely boyfriend. They were a sweet couple and fit into our group so naturally. But it didn't stop there.

Soon I met Giada, a real pocket rocket. Loud, funny, and delightfully crazy. Around her, it was impossible to be in a bad mood.

She worked at a crêpe and ice cream shop right in the middle of town, and we became regulars there too. Not just because they had the best ice cream and fluffiest crêpes, but also because we never had to pay. Giada spoiled us every day with sweet treats while she stood behind the counter with her wide smile, laughing loudly and lighting up everyone around her.

Our little girls' crew had now become a proper unit – made up of Michela, the cheerful Italian with the contagious laugh; Giulia, my soul friend, always there with open arms and the biggest heart; Fede, half German, half Italian, with her cool, easygoing vibe – finally someone I could speak German with every now and then; and of course Giada, our colourful whirlwind with an ice cream cone in hand and wild ideas in her head.

We experienced so many unforgettable things together – spontaneous trips, long talks on the beach, laughter, pizza, and of course, plenty of tiramisu.

As I soaked it all in, I realised: this is what makes travelling so special. Not just the places, but especially the people you meet along the way.

If you're currently thinking about travelling alone – do it. Don't wait for someone to come with you. Don't wait for the perfect moment, the perfect plan, or the perfect travel buddy. Just go.

Yes, it takes courage. But often, that first step into the unknown is the beginning of something big. Travelling alone doesn't mean being lonely. Quite the opposite – sometimes you're never more open to connection than in those moments when you're completely with yourself. The best conversations, the most unexpected twists, the deepest feelings often happen when you simply dare to let go. When you trust life without a safety net.

You'll be surprised how often you'll meet people you never would've encountered otherwise, simply because you were travelling alone. You'll learn that you don't need anyone else to feel whole. And you'll be amazed by the clarity that can rise within you when there's no one around to distract you. It might be exactly what you need to discover what you truly want.

Even though I was surrounded by new, wonderful people every day, I kept catching myself thinking about my old group. I missed them – those special people who had made everything feel so effortless.

So often I wished I could just see a familiar face, give someone a quick hug and ask,

*»So, how are you? What's life been like?«*

Instead, there were now other voices, other stories – beautiful in their own way, but not my people.

Australia is huge. So huge, in fact, that you could theoretically fit Germany into it 21 times without it overflowing. And yet, this continent can sometimes feel like a tiny village, especially when you're backpacking.

You travel all over the country, say what you think is a final goodbye to someone, only to bump into them three weeks later at a remote beach kiosk while ordering a smoothie. That's why, deep down, I still hoped that fate would bring me one last reunion. Sometime. Somewhere.

Amidst that longing, I began to crave moments that belonged only to me. Little islands of calm in the chaos of backpacker life.

I grabbed my headphones, put on my favourite songs – the kind that automatically make you walk half a step slower, and set off for Tallow Beach. My own personal retreat. I wanted to clear my head, stare out at the ocean, breathe deeply, feel the sun on my face and figure out what I really wanted. What made me happy. What I expected from the rest of my time in Australia – and, more fundamentally, what I actually wanted from life.

The day was quiet, almost meditative. Until, as so often in Australia, I was once again reminded that life tends to shout *»Surprise!«,* just when you think nothing else will happen.

I was walking along a sandy shoulder by the road, lost in thought, when suddenly a car horn blared. Loud. Joyful. Impossible to ignore. I nearly jumped out of my skin. My heart slipped right into my flip-flops.

I turned around, and then something happened that I never in my life would have expected. A familiar face grinned at me from the open car window. I squinted. No bloody way. But yes. It was Nici. Yes, that Nici!

The Nici I'd spent so many weeks and months travelling with. My first instinct was to burst out laughing. My second impulse was to shout at him and ask if he'd completely lost his mind, scaring me like that. But deep down, something entirely different took over: a huge, warm wave of joy. I couldn't believe it.

He'd seen my story on Instagram and wanted to surprise me, but his phone battery had died because he'd slept in the car, and now here he was, standing right in front of me. I ran toward him, threw myself into his arms, and just started crying. Tears of joy, relief, and pure emotion. I didn't want to let go. It felt like coming home.

Nici wasn't alone. He had two new friends with him—Ludwig and Samuel, or just Sam. Both were from Germany and had travelled with him from Bundaberg to Byron Bay for a few days, where they were currently doing farm work. The distance? Over 500 kilometres! More than six hours of driving. Just to spend a weekend in Byron Bay. Someone who does that must really love this place... or maybe, just maybe—also the people who are there.

⁓

We spontaneously decided to spend the whole weekend together, and it turned out to be one of the best. We drove to White's Beach, that hidden paradise you can only reach by climbing down many steep steps.

We swam in the waves, lay in the sun, and laughed like we used to. Everything was there. Everything was back again. That indescribable feeling of freedom, connection, and home. My 'social battery', which sometimes drained faster than expected, was completely recharged during those days. Seeing Nici again, talking to him, having his energy around me — it was like balm for the soul. It reminded me of how everything had once begun and that some connections are simply meant to last.

One sunny afternoon, Nici, Sam, Ludwig and I decided to treat ourselves to some fish and chips. We grabbed our meals from Fishheads, a popular restaurant right on Byron Bay's Main Beach, and found a spot on the wide grassy area in front of the beach, lined with palm trees and offering a beautiful view of the ocean. No sooner had we sat down and taken our first bite than we were ambushed by a flock of seagulls. These feathered thieves circled above us, landed nearby and stared us down with piercing eyes. Some of them were even bold enough to come so close they tried snatching chips straight from our hands. We ended up having to defend our food in what became a comical battle between humans and birds. Despite the unexpected challenge, we enjoyed our lunch and soaked in the relaxed atmosphere.

The sun was warm on our skin, the sound of the waves provided a calming backdrop, and our laughter over the ridiculous situation with the seagulls echoed across the grass.

That evening, we made our way to a beach party. The atmosphere was lively, music blaring from portable speakers, and groups of people danced barefoot in the sand.

It was obvious, though, that some of the guests were under the influence of various substances. Their movements were uncoordinated, their conversations all over the place. Still, we enjoyed the evening, danced, laughed, and let ourselves be carried away by the energy of the night. It was another unforgettable day in Byron, shaped by simple pleasures, unexpected encounters, and the realisation that true happiness often lies in the small, clear moments.

After saying goodbye to Nici and his two friends the next day, things settled down a bit again.

My girls' group – Michela, Giulia, and Fede, completely understood that I had spent the weekend with old friends. It felt like I had somehow connected two worlds – the past and the present.

A few days later, we suddenly felt the urge to try something completely "new." Something a bit wild, a bit daring, and somehow also very European.

Giulia, Michela, and I were just sitting in the hostel garden when, during one of those typical girl chats, someone suddenly said:

*»Don't you think we should just go skinny dipping?«*

My German friends and family would probably smirk at this — for us, it's nothing too wild. Nudist beaches are kind of part of the culture in Germany. You basically grow up surrounded by bare bums at the local pool or lake. No one even turns their head. But in Australia? Well… nudity at the beach is a bit more of a sensitive topic. It's not a complete no-go, but it's definitely not something people do casually. Especially not in public.

Still, we had made up our minds. We wanted to go through with it. Skinny dipping in Australia, just to see how it feels to swim in the waves in complete freedom, without a bikini getting in the way.

Our destination: Kings Beach — a remote, hidden little beach near Byron Bay, known for its relaxed vibe and the fact that now and then, someone might go for a dip without their swimmers and not end up in jail for it.

Getting there was a bit of an adventure in itself, it was a narrow path through dense greenery, almost like trekking through the jungle. When we finally reached the beach, we were instantly blown away by the untouched nature and incredible stillness. Not a soul in sight. Perfect conditions for our little experiment.

At first, we felt a bit awkward. It was our first time at a nude beach, and even though we encouraged each other, it still took a little courage. It felt like we had to push past our own hesitation... or more accurately: past our own towel.

But then, a short moment of doubt, one last look, a collective

*»Alright, now or never!«,*

and suddenly we were standing there — naked and free, the sun on our skin, the sand beneath our feet, and the ocean in front of us. It was a feeling of lightness that's hard to describe. Almost like, for just a moment, we had let go of everything, literally and figuratively.

That moment reminded me how important it is to stay open to new experiences and to challenge yourself. Sometimes, the greatest adventures lie in pushing past your own limits and diving into the unknown.

∽

Time was slipping away faster than I liked. Each day felt like a small, precious goodbye.

I knew my flight was approaching – the return to Germany was already booked, and my visa would soon expire. I had about a month left. Four more weeks in my beloved Australia before I'd return to the life I once left behind. Of course, I was looking forward to seeing my family. It had been almost a year and a half since I'd last seen them.

The thought of finally hugging my mum again, sitting on the couch with her, sharing stories and simply being close in a familiar space, made my heart soften. I was also really looking forward to seeing my dad – our little rituals, like having a slice of cake together on his balcony, laughing, talking for hours, and just losing track of time. But it wasn't just my parents I missed. I missed my entire family. My stepdad, my grandma, grandparents, my brother and his wife, my quirky aunt – all the familiar voices and faces that had always been part of my life. It was that feeling of home that showed itself in all the little things: a shared breakfast, a family gathering, or simply sitting in silence together.

And then, of course, there were my friends – people who had been by my side for years, who knew my wildest sides, who had laughed and cried with me and shared countless memories. I couldn't wait to see them again. To finally hug them properly, not just wave through a video call. I had missed them, more than I sometimes wanted to admit.

Still, despite all this anticipation, the thought of saying goodbye to Australia just didn't feel right. Deep down, I wasn't ready to close this chapter yet. I wasn't ready yet—not ready to shake the sand of Byron Bay from my shoes or to trade the ocean for everyday life. I wanted to make the most of the time I had left, savouring all the little moments that made daily life there so special.

But another farewell was also drawing closer. One that hit me even harder: saying goodbye to our car—Goldie. Our car. Our home on wheels. Our refuge in the rain, in the wind, in the heat. Letting go of it felt almost as painful as parting with a person. That might sound exaggerated to some, but anyone who's ever travelled through a foreign country in an old car knows the kind of bond that can form. Goldie wasn't just a vehicle. It was our companion across thousands of kilometres, through dust and sunshine, through highs and lows. It had been mine and Nati's adventure on four wheels, and now, with a heavy heart, it was time to let go.

So I put up an ad, and just a few days later, a young couple reached out. Of course—Italians. How could it have been any other way during this Byron Bay chapter, which seemed to be blessed by an Italian star.

The two of them were looking for a reliable car for their own Australian adventure, and Goldie was a perfect match. I knew they would take good care of it, I could feel it straight away. Still, the day I sold it was one of the hardest. I still remember clearly how they slowly drove off with the car. I stood there, watching as Goldie turned the corner, and suddenly a wave of emotion overwhelmed me.

In that moment, I realised how many memories were tied to that car. How many sunrises we had watched from inside it. How many nights we'd spent lying in our little bed in the boot, the back hatch open, the fresh air in our lungs – while above us, the sky was full of stars. We'd lie there for hours, talking about life, our dreams, our worries. I never thought a piece of metal could mean so much to me. Saying goodbye to Goldie stirred up more inside me than I wanted to admit at first. I needed a moment to process it all – and, as so often before, I was drawn to the only place that always made my heart feel lighter: Tallow Beach.

This time, I actually made it there without anyone honking at me or surprising me out of nowhere. I hadn't seen it in so long – my favourite beach. That long, endless stretch of soft white sand, nestled between lush eucalyptus forests on one side and the vast turquoise sea on the other. The ocean roared with power, almost majestic, while the wind gently rustled through the treetops above me. It was one of those places that didn't just feel like nature, it felt like peace.

I sat down in the sand and pulled a small necklace from my pocket, one I had bought that morning for barely ten dollars. A delicate pendant in the shape of a tiny glass bottle. So simple, yet filled with so much meaning. I instantly knew what I wanted to do with it. Carefully, I filled it with a bit of sand – maybe a millilitre, if that. But to me, it was everything. A tangible memory of this very special place. A place that had held me so many times. Where I had fallen most in love with surfing. Where Amira got stung by a stingray and still carried on with a smile. Where I had walked for miles – barefoot, hair blowing in the wind, salty skin, lost in thought, completely alive. Where my life had been saved, and I had truly felt free.

I sealed the tiny bottle and held it in my hand for a while. It was my personal keepsake, a farewell gift to myself. Not an expensive souvenir from a shop, but a tiny piece of Australia that would stay with me forever. A piece of my heart, in a little glass vial.

After spending the day alone at Tallow Beach, I stayed for a long time, feet buried in the warm sand, eyes fixed on the endless sea. I wanted to soak in every moment, every breath, every wave rolling onto the shore. I knew I wouldn't come back here again. Not in this time, not in this chapter of my life, and this place, this very special place, would live on in my heart exactly as I saw it now.

When I got back to the hostel later, my favourite girls were already waiting with excited faces. Michela, Giada, Giulia and Fede had planned something—a little road trip. Their last. My last.

And you won't believe it, our destination was Fraser Island! Or rather: K'gari. I didn't hesitate for long. What did I have to lose? Exactly, nothing. But so much to gain.

A few more days of adventure, laughter, sunsets, sandy feet and windblown hair. I wanted to soak it all in one more time, savour every single day before my flight back to Germany.

So I said yes. Yes to one more little chapter that felt just right.

I packed my things, grabbed my backpack from the corner, stuffed in my bathers, sunscreen and good vibes, and off we went. Off to Fraser Island. Off to freedom. Off to memories. Even the drive there made me grin. I remembered my first trip to K'gari, back then with Nati and Eric. How we drove for hours along the beach, windows down, music loud, and how our tyre suddenly blew out in the middle of nowhere. And how, at the campsite that night, those giant goannas, like mini dinosaurs, almost gave us a heart attack as they crept out of the bushes in silence, prowling for food around the tents.

This second road trip was nothing like the first, but it was just as special. With Michela, Giulia, Giada and Fede, I experienced Fraser Island—K'gari, in a whole new way. This island, the largest sand island in the world, felt like another universe. The crystal-clear lakes, endless sand tracks, tropical bushland and wild animals roaming the campsites at night. Being there again felt almost surreal.

We explored the island in our own way. Drove along the famous 75 Mile Beach, stopped at viewpoints, laughed, sang in the car and let the wind tangle our hair. Of course, we couldn't miss Lake McKenzie, that turquoise freshwater lake with its snow-white sand was still just as magical as the first time. We swam in the crystal-clear water, then lay in the shade of the trees and even had a little nap. The sun above us, the soft rustling of the wind in the branches. I'd seen much of it before, but it didn't matter. This time everything felt new, because of the people I shared it with. Their energy, their joy, our conversations – all of it made the trip something truly unique.

It was a five-day road trip that felt like a little summer movie. In the early mornings, we'd crawl out of our tents, slip into our flip-flops, and walk through the scrub straight down to the beach, where the sun slowly rose over the ocean. Those moments, when the first light of day touched the waves, they made you forget that somewhere out there, a return flight was waiting.

After taking the ferry back to the mainland, we spontaneously decided to top off our road trip with one final highlight: Movie World, a theme park on the Gold Coast, just south of Brisbane.

It's known for its film sets, rollercoasters, and shows featuring Warner Bros. characters – a mix of adrenaline, nostalgia, and pure entertainment. Between Superman, Scooby-Doo, and wild rides in the sun, we laughed until our stomachs hurt. It was a completely different kind of day than the ones on the island, but just as special.

After the colourful chaos of the park, we made our way back to Byron Bay. And even though everything was slowly coming to an end, my heart was still so full of warmth that it didn't feel like saying goodbye, more like the final chapter of a perfect book you never want to close.

∿

My final five days in Byron Bay had begun. Back at the YHA hostel, it felt as though the circle had closed.

In the evenings we cooked together, sat barefoot on the wooden benches in the courtyard, played cards or listened to music from small Bluetooth speakers lying somewhere between surfboards and backpacks. Everything felt familiar again. I knew these were my last sunsets in Byron, my final breakfast in the hostel kitchen, my last jump into the waves at Main Beach. And in these final days, I met someone new: Natalia. A quiet yet witty soul with a mix of Russian and German roots.

Her parents were from Russia, she spoke both languages fluently, and she was bursting with energy. Natalia worked in housekeeping at the hostel, cleaning rooms to fund her stay in Byron. A typical backpacker job – not forever, but enough to soak up a few more months under the sun.

One evening, just as we came back from a surf session with wet hair and salty skin, we were suddenly approached.

A photographer who had been staying at the hostel for days came over to us. Apparently, he'd seen us a few times at the beach, walking through the dunes with boards under our arms, laughing.

He said he'd love to photograph us. He had a professional camera setup, an old van filled with his gear, and wanted to do a free shoot for a personal project to use in his portfolio. Of course, we could keep the pictures too. Natalia and I didn't need long to think about it. Surf photos on the beach? Why not.

The very next morning, he picked us up in his van, and we drove together to one of my favourite beaches: Wategos Beach. A little paradise tucked between hills and rocks, where the water sparkles turquoise and the sun casts a golden shimmer over the waves – that is, if you're lucky enough to find a parking spot.

As I grabbed my surfboard and walked barefoot across the warm sand towards the sea, he started taking photos. The sun was low, the light was perfect, and then it happened: right behind me, just metres away, dolphins suddenly appeared. They were surfing the wave that was breaking directly behind me, and the photographer hit the shutter at the exact right moment.

That one photo – the one I now use as the cover of this book, was captured right then and there. No posing. No planning. Just pure luck, and life. I remember standing there, speechless, board in hand, thinking: if that's not a sign…

I'd often wondered how I would leave this place – what kind of feeling I'd take with me, and then life simply gifted me this moment.

We spent the rest of the day taking photos in the water, surfing, with salt in our hair and sand between our toes. The photographer also had an underwater camera with him, and that's how we captured some unforgettable shots — pictures I now treasure like gold. It felt as though Byron Bay had given me one last special moment before saying goodbye, wrapped in saltwater, sunshine, and the quiet magic of a place that would forever be part of me.

My second-last day in Australia had come. Like so many backpackers before me, I spent it in a chaotic mix of farewell emotions, frantic organising, and sentimental thoughts. I sat in my room for hours, trying to squeeze all my stuff into my backpack — or rather, into two backpacks. My carry-on, and somehow also my longboard, which I'd ordered a few weeks earlier while I was in Orange. Back then, I'd thought,

*»I don't want to keep borrowing one from someone else.«*
Now I was thinking,
*»How am I supposed to get all this to the airport on my own?«*

It was a sight to behold. I sat there in the middle of the chaos, surrounded by clothes, seashells, sunscreen, a ukulele, souvenirs, shoes, and memories — laughing out loud at myself. At everything I'd somehow collected over the past one and a half years.

*»How did I set off with just one backpack and now end up standing here with four bags?«*

Especially in Byron Bay, with its endless little shops full of charm and detail, it was impossible not to give in every now and then. The people, the atmosphere, the colours, even a simple ring or dress suddenly carried meaning here.

Once I'd finally managed to pack everything, I realised one important thing was still missing from my to-do list: There was no way I could leave Byron without getting one last little tattoo.

There's a tattoo studio in town where you can just walk in without an appointment — and that's exactly what I did, together with Giulia, who didn't want a needle near her but happily came along for moral support.

I got two new pieces inked as memories: a tiny wave on the side of my foot — a symbol of all the hours I'd spent in the water, and a small moon on one finger, directly opposite the mini sun I already had on the other.

To me, they weren't just tattoos. They were visible chapters of my life. Marks on my skin that would always whisper:

»*You lived. You were brave. You were free*«.

That evening, our entire group gathered one last time. Michela had booked a huge table at the restaurant. We all sat together — talking, laughing, sharing memories. Everyone knew it was my last night, and that's exactly why they had all come. It wasn't loud or over the top – more warm, familiar, honest. Just like everything in Byron Bay, when you've found friends who feel like family.

I could've stayed there forever. My heart felt heavy, even though I knew I was flying home, back to my family and my friends in Germany. Of course, I was looking forward to seeing them again, hearing familiar voices, and finally hugging people I had known before this whole journey began. But deep down, I also knew: I wasn't ready. Not yet. The timing felt off, but I didn't have a choice. My visa was about to expire, and I'd made a conscious decision not to use my second one just yet.

The borders to Western Australia were still closed, and I wanted to save that option, to one day explore that side of the country too. Spending another year on the East Coast didn't feel right for me. So it was settled: back to Germany for now. Without a plan for what I'd do there. No clue how things would unfold. But with one clear intention: To come back.

That evening, surrounded by these wonderful people, good food, and fairy lights strung above the table, became my perfect little farewell. No big drama. Just a quiet, glowing thank you, to a country that had changed my life.

Then I woke up one last time in my beloved Byron Bay. The final day had arrived, the day my flight would leave. It wasn't until late in the afternoon, but I knew I wanted to have this morning all to myself. One last time waking up with the comforting thought: I'm still here. One last time to breathe, to feel, to see.

The evening before, I had already made my decision: I would spend my final sunrise at the Cape Byron Lighthouse – a place that was so much more than just a lookout. It was a place full of memories. Of Nati, Marzio, Nici, and all the encounters, all the conversations, the laughter, the tears, the dreams. This place was soaked with emotion, woven with moments that had shaped me.

At 3:30 a.m., my alarm rang. It was pitch black. I got dressed quietly, slung my small backpack over my shoulder, and left the hostel. The streets were completely still, only the distant sound of the ocean could be heard. I had my headphones in, but there was only one song I wanted to hear: "Heaven" by Ziggy Alberts. A song that might mean nothing to others, but for me, it had become one of the most powerful soundtracks of my life. Every time I hear that song now, I'm instantly transported back to that moment – walking alone toward the lighthouse, eyes fixed ahead, while the sky slowly turned a soft shade of orange.

When I reached the top, I stood at the edge of the world. The lighthouse glowed against the pale morning sky, and in front of me stretched the vast, endless blue of the Pacific Ocean. To my left I saw 'The Pass', to my right my beloved 'Tallow Beach'.

The first rays of sunlight kissed the waves, and the water began to shimmer. Dolphins swam along the coastline below, riding the waves as if they were there to say goodbye. I stood there for over an hour, without saying a word, taking no photos, and just looking out at the sea and the horizon. At my Australia.

My heart felt like it was about to burst. It was as if a thousand tiny shards were breaking away, while I realised that this chapter of my life was now coming to an end. Not forever. But for now.

It was my film, and I was the main character. But the credits had begun to roll. Never before had a place felt so much like home, so much like myself – and now I was supposed to leave it behind. Yet in that exact moment, alone with the rising sun, the song in my ears, the salty air on my skin, and the certainty that I would never forget this place, I was also filled with deep gratitude. Because I had been lucky enough to experience it.

When I returned from the lighthouse, that very special morning was behind me – my final morning in Australia.

The sun was already high in the sky when I met up one last time for breakfast with my dear Giulia and her friend Erica, who – with her gentle and kind nature, had quickly found a place in my heart. We sat outside under palm trees, letting the sun warm our faces as we had breakfast together. I still remember exactly how warm the air felt, how the quiet giggles from other guests drifted past us, and how hard I tried to breathe in that moment—so deeply, as if I could somehow store it within me.

But even the most beautiful morning eventually comes to an end.

In the early afternoon, the two of them took me to the small Ballina Byron Gateway Airport—one of the most charming, tiniest airports I've ever seen. Barely bigger than a basketball court, with only a few gates, short walking distances, and a tiny café. But suddenly, that place felt enormous, because it meant goodbye.

As we stood in the car park and I hugged them both tightly one last time, I couldn't stop crying. I knew I was leaving Australia—the country where, for the first time, I had felt completely free, real, and alive. A country that had changed me. Even though I was looking forward to seeing my family, there was this huge ache in my chest.

*»Why was I leaving a place that finally felt like home?«*

I couldn't give myself a clear answer. And when I finally walked through the glass doors and waved to Giulia and Erica one last time, I felt it: Now it's really over.

I looked back, trying to memorise their smiles, then turned around with tears in my eyes. The wait at the airport felt like it dragged on forever. I sat there with my backpack, my longboard, all my luggage, but the heaviest weight I carried was my emotions. The tears just wouldn't stop.

A security guard even came over, gently bent down and asked with genuine concern in her voice:

*»Are you okay, love?«*

I could only shake my head. Then she said with a soft smile:

*»Why don't you just stay? You could even work here, if you want«*

I gave a faint nod, too overwhelmed to respond. But that one sentence, that casual remark, became a key moment in my life – even though I didn't know it yet. It would change everything.

A little while later, a woman who worked at the airport café quietly approached me. Without saying a word, she placed a bottle of water on the table in front of me, along with two packets of tissues.

She'd seen me from afar – sitting there, lost, overwhelmed, and heartbroken. It was one of the hardest goodbyes of my life, and yet... also one of the most meaningful.

When I finally boarded the plane and sat in my seat under the dim cabin light, it hit me with full force: This was it. My greatest adventure had begun — and now, it was over. Australia, the country that had saved me, changed me, challenged me and healed me, lay beneath me as the plane lifted off. As so often, I got lucky again, with a window seat. It felt almost like a sign. I'd hoped so much to get one last glimpse from above of this country that had stolen my heart. One last look at Australia. One last look at the place that had come to feel like home.

Below me stretched the coastline – long, golden, glistening. I recognised Byron Bay. I saw Tallow Beach, the lighthouse, the familiar curves of the coast. The sun bathed everything in a soft orange glow, reflecting off the ocean as if the sky had dressed up one last time to say goodbye. It didn't feel real. I was flying away, from my favourite place on Earth, from this new version of myself. And then, as if Australia had thought,

*»Alright, let's hit her where it hurts,«*

a song suddenly started playing on my playlist. Not selected, not planned. It just came on. "Happiest Year" by Jaymes Young began. The very first lines made me freeze:

*»I never should have said goodbye, but maybe that's what stupid people do...«*

And then that one line that broke me:

*»Thank you for the happiest year of my life.«*

I stared out of the window. In front of me: the light, the ocean, the sky — and my final glimpse of Australia. I cried harder than I had in a long time. Out of pain. Out of gratitude. Because I could feel it: a part of me would forever remain here. Along these coasts, on these roads, between red sand dunes and turquoise waters. In all the encounters, the hugs, and the goodbyes. In the salty air, the quiet nights by the campfire, and the loud moments of pure life.

Australia hadn't just been a place. It was a chapter of my life that changed me. A teacher, a mirror, a temporary home. I had come here to turn my life upside down, and I did. I failed, I grew, I fell, and got back up again. I made friendships that will last a lifetime. I laughed, cried, loved, let go, found myself, or at least saw myself clearly for the first time. Australia showed me how little you actually need to be truly happy. It taught me how to travel alone, but never feel lonely. It taught me to be brave, to make decisions, even when they hurt. It taught me that freedom is sometimes just a matter of perspective. I learned to allow pauses. To trust — in myself, in life. I learned that home doesn't have to be a place, but a feeling. And sometimes, that feeling is born thousands of kilometres away.

This country didn't just welcome me, it shaped me. And now, it was letting me go, with one last sunset and all the memories no one could ever take away from me.

*Thank you, Australia.*
*For the best chapter of my life.*

# CHAPTER TWENTY TWO
## HOME COMING

The flight felt endless. My body had lost all sense of how many hours I had already been awake. All I knew was this: I was flying back to a country I would never see the same way again.

As we flew over Germany, all I could see was white. Everything was frozen, snow-covered fields stretched out below me, and with every kilometre, my heart grew a little heavier. I was coming from warm, wild, free Australia... and heading back to a world that suddenly felt unfamiliar.

We landed in Berlin. Not exactly a pretty sight from above – flat, cold, grey. No sunrise over the ocean, no palm trees, no red sandy roads, no dolphins anywhere. Just asphalt and ice. Still, my heart was pounding. I was excited because I knew my family and friends would be there waiting.

But as I stepped off the plane and found myself surrounded by Germans again for the first time, the culture shock hit me hard: grey faces, no one smiling. Everyone looked stern, rushed, serious.

In that moment, I knew: I didn't belong here anymore. This place, this country… it was no longer my home.

But I tried to look ahead. Because I knew: in just a few minutes, I would see my family again. My friends. My mum. And then, it happened. I came through the glass doors with my luggage, my vision still blurred from all the thoughts, and then I saw them. All of them. Holding a huge sign in their hands, painted with big, lovingly drawn letters:

*»Welcome Home«*

Next to it: a little Bluetooth speaker playing "I'm Coming Home" at exactly that moment. I stopped. For a moment, everything seemed to freeze. A hundred eyes turned toward us—passengers, bystanders, airport staff. But I didn't care. Because there they were: my people.

My mum was the first to run towards me, tears in her eyes, arms wide open. I dropped my luggage, fell into her arms, and cried. I had longed for this moment so much—for her scent, her voice, her warmth. And at the same time… I cried for Australia. For the country I had to leave behind. For all the memories that had shaped me forever. It was everything at once: joy, pain, gratitude, overwhelm, love. A tsunami of emotions, and I was right in the middle of it. Torn between two worlds, but endlessly grateful to have experienced both.

It wasn't Germany that felt like home anymore, but the

hugs, the voices, the familiarity of my family and friends. That was home. In their arms, I found that feeling again, the one I had missed for so long. The country around me no longer felt like the place I belonged. But they did. And that was enough, for now.

∿

We drove home. I was exhausted, the jet lag was pounding in my head. I wouldn't see the rest of my family and friends until the next day – I simply didn't have the energy. Also, it was freezing. I could feel the cold creeping into my bones. My breath formed little clouds in front of my face. I was shivering. Not just on the outside, deep inside, too. I was back. But I hadn't truly arrived.

Over the next few days, I visited the rest of my family. I spent time with my dad, sitting on the balcony like we used to, eating a slice of cake together. I saw my grandmas and my grandpa, my brother and his wife, my aunt, my cousin, and my friends. Everyone was excited. I was hugged, asked a hundred questions, welcomed home.

Of course I was happy, I had longed to see them all again. But somehow… something was missing.

With each passing day, it became more obvious: as much as I love my family, I hadn't really arrived. Not fully. I walked through German streets and saw grey faces, empty expressions. No one smiled. People seemed irritated, rushed, dissatisfied. I kept asking myself:

*»Was I really born here?«*

The contrast to Australia couldn't have been bigger. There, strangers had helped me without expecting anything in return. They had shown genuine interest, opened doors without hidden agendas. There was no suspicion, no jealousy, no constant complaining. People celebrated one another's joy, and not against it.

Here, on the other hand, kindness seemed almost suspicious. Willingness to help was rare. Openness was seen as naivety. I felt like I had stumbled back into the wrong life. Like I was in a body that no longer fit. As if I'd put on an old costume that didn't suit me anymore.

You return changed, but everything around you is still the same. The same streets. The same conversations. The same problems. Only you… you've become someone completely different. You've seen too much, lived too much, changed too much. You've let go, trusted, laughed, doubted, and learned. And suddenly, you no longer fit into the life you once left behind.

I tried to reorient myself. I started looking for a job. Thought about what should come next. But the more I tried to fit in, the more foreign everything felt. Slowly, almost imperceptibly, I slipped into a void. An inner silence that weighed heavily on me. What kept me going was this one thought that kept coming back, clear and anchored deep within me:

*»When can I go back to Australia?«*


That thought became my anchor. It grounded me when nothing else did. Because part of me was still there, between the waves, under the sun, in moments that had shaped me like no other place ever had.

The hardest part wasn't leaving. The hardest part was coming back. Because while everything here had stayed the same, I had changed. Quietly. Deeply. Irrevocably. Home was still there, but it no longer felt like mine.

And so this quiet question lingered within me:

*»Where do I belong now?«*

Germany felt like a place where time had stood still, while my world had long moved on. Everything was just as I had left it. And that was exactly why I had left. The idea that this was now supposed to be my life, that thought was almost unbearable. A life in which I'd always leave, only to eventually return to a reality that never truly felt right?

Even if I could go back to Australia for another year, then what? Would I end up here again, in a country that no longer fit me? Would I walk the same streets again, see the same faces, and once again wonder why I came back?

Even back then, a decision had started to form inside me. A decision that felt enormous. Maybe extreme — but true. And to this day, I have never regretted it. I probably never will. Because I knew: I didn't just want to return to Australia for another year. I wanted to stay forever, and leave Germany behind for good.

Not out of anger or hate. But because my heart had long begun to live elsewhere. Australia had become my home.

The thought of returning to Germany only as a visitor was no longer something I feared, it had become a goal. A future I could truly wish for.

That thought circled in my mind for months. Sometimes quietly in the background, sometimes so loud it drowned everything else out. But I had no idea how to explain it to the people who had been part of my life forever.

How do you tell those who love you that you want to say goodbye to the place they still call "home"?

How do you explain that, deep down, you've already moved on – even though you're still physically here?

Only my mum knew. She had sensed it. The way mothers just know when something starts to shift within their child. She knows me better than anyone. Even before I said it out loud, she could see it in my eyes. She knew I wasn't truly happy here anymore. That my heart was already beating somewhere across the ocean. And even though she would miss me, she wanted exactly that for me: a life where I could be truly free and happy. One not shaped by expectations or routines, but by who I really am.

Maybe it wouldn't happen tomorrow. Maybe not next week, maybe not even this year. But some decisions don't need a deadline. No exact date, no perfect explanation. Sometimes, all it takes is a feeling. A single thought. Quiet, barely noticeable, until it plants itself deep inside you and begins to grow. Until you can't ignore it anymore. Until that thought becomes a direction. And that direction turns into an irreversible decision.

Because when a place touches you so deeply that you can't get it out of your heart, then it's not just a place. It's a part of you. Maybe even the part that's been missing all these years.

I'm coming back. Not for a trip. Not for a chapter. But for a life that has been waiting for me far longer than I ever knew.

# Epilogue

They say that at some point in life, there comes a moment when you don't just find a place — you find yourself. Australia was that place for me.

Byron Bay, that dreamy little coastal paradise, became more than just a stop along my journey. It became my turning point. My healing. My home far away from everything I once knew. I arrived feeling lost, and I left knowing who I truly am. I loved, laughed, learned, cried, let go, and held on. I made lifelong friendships, slept in the sand, dreamed under the stars and found myself in the glow of countless sunrises.

The decision to leave was the hardest of my life. Because how do you walk away from something that feels so deeply right? How do you say goodbye to a place that showed you you're enough, just as you are?

But sometimes, you have to let go to make room for what's meant to come. To see paths that were hidden in the fog. To close circles, or begin new ones. Sometimes, you have to release the old life to make space for the new.

That final glance from the plane window felt like a quiet promise. A part of my heart stayed behind, in the salty sea breeze and the crashing waves, in surfboards resting in the sand and the shimmer of tropical waterfalls, in humpback whales breaching in the distance and dolphins swimming beside me, in goggles and campfires, sunrises and freedom. In the space between who I was, and the life I finally allowed myself to feel.

*And who knows?*
*Maybe one day the wind will carry me home again.*

*Anne Janko, Western Australia, August 2025*

www.ingramcontent.com/pod-product-compliance
Lightning Source LLC
Chambersburg PA
CBHW022334300426
44109CB00040B/723